Delivered From
DEMON
POSSESSION

By Vaughn Allen

TEACH Services, Inc.
P U B L I S H I N G
www.TEACHServices.com • (800) 367-1844

Facsimile Reproduction

As this book played a formative role in the development of Christian thought and the publisher feels that this book, with its candor and depth, still holds significance for the church today. Therefore the publisher has chosen to reproduce this historical classic from an original copy. Frequent variations in the quality of the print are unavoidable due to the condition of the original. Thus the print may look darker or lighter or appear to be missing detail, more in some places than in others.

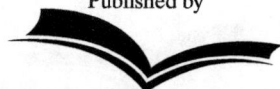

Copyright © 2023 TEACH Services, Inc.
ISBN-13: 978-1-4796-1664-0 (Paperback)

Published by

TEACH Services, Inc.
P U B L I S H I N G
www.TEACHServices.com • (800) 367-1844

Dear Reader:

As you read the story recorded on these pages, you will become acquainted with me as Paula Green. However, Paula Green is not my true name. For reasons which you will understand, I prefer not to use my real name.

I have read the author's manuscript, and I certify that the events described in these pages really happened as recorded here, insofar as I am able to remember. Brief interludes occurred that summer when I was not fully aware of my actions or completely conscious of my surroundings because at that time other powers were controlling my mind.

In the hope that others who read of my experience will be spared from a similar one, I have given permission to make my story known. In this way I want to praise God for the wonderful deliverance He has given me. To Him I give all the glory!

Paula Green

Preface

Demon possession is becoming more prevalent. Have you ever witnessed someone under the control of evil spirits? If so, then these chapters will especially interest you. If you have never had such an experience, then I urge you to read this book; for the time may come, even sooner than you may think, when you will be called upon to help someone under the harassment of demonic powers.

A few years ago Pacific Press urged me to make available something of my own experience with the occult, which resulted in the book *Secrets of the Spirit World*. Knowing I had faced demonic powers in a number of different countries, Pastor Vaughn Allen invited me to share with him the burden and responsibility of Paula's problem. One who has faced the enemy of God and man is never eager to drive head on into the powers of Satan. Nevertheless, I consented to do what I could to help the young woman of this story.

To see an otherwise quiet Christian lady under such power is a repulsive sight which becomes even uglier when one hears the coarse, raucous voice of a supernatural power, with curses and challenges to the living God, speaking through the very one we are trying to help.

I want to assure you that what you read is all true. This is not a novel. It is a stirring, accurate report of what happened time and time again until finally deliverance came.

Pastor Vaughn Allen is an experienced educator, having carried responsibility for hundreds of academy youth during some twenty-five years. He is now associate pastor of one of our churches in southern California. During these intensive days, a number of leaders and members united in importunate prayer, claiming victory for Paula, and our prayers were answered through Jesus Christ, our Saviour and Lord. To Him be the praise.

Roy Allen Anderson

Author's Preface

The story I am about to relate is so unusual that you may find it hard to believe. All of the events portrayed here took place within a five-week period, from the last day of June until the first week in August. During that time I saw God cast eight demons out of the body and mind of a young woman whom I shall call Paula Green, although that is not her real name.

I want to assure you that I personally observed these events just as I have recorded them here. Of the several people who were involved in this experience, I am the only one who witnessed the entire series of events from beginning to end. Others were present at one or more of the "encounters," depending upon the time and circumstances. Elder R. Allen Anderson, well-known denominational leader and author, was present during several of these encounters. Pastor William Doyle and his wife were present at the all-day session on Thursday, and Pastor Doyle participated in several confrontations on other days. Next to myself, Pastor Andrew Paddock, our youth pastor, participated in the largest number of these confrontations. He was present on Thursday, and he witnessed several other encounters.

Kenneth and Dorothy Stiles were also present when several of the encounters took place, including the last ones, which were the most prolonged and severe. Kenneth is a retired church-school administrator and teacher and an elder in my church. Both he and Dorothy have also served as missionaries in Africa. My wife was present at two confrontations, including the first one; and our older daughter was involved in one of them.

During this five-week period eighteen or twenty confrontations occurred, and at each of these encounters the demons spoke. I have recorded their words verbatim, or nearly so. They were so deeply impressed upon my mind that it won't be easy to forget them. After the first encounter, I thought of recording these "conversations" on tape. But I decided against this because I could think of nothing that would be gained by it, and I was afraid that it might impede or even defeat the purpose of the confrontations.

I have two reasons for relating this experience. First, I want in this way to praise God for the wonderful thing He did in banishing the demons from Paula's mind and body and for transforming her life so completely.

Second, I believe God's people should be as informed as possible about Satan's methods of operation. Ellen White has written, "There is nothing that the great deceiver fears as much as that we shall become acquainted with his devices."—*The Great Controversy*, p. 516. I believe that from the experiences related here many can gain some insight as to his "devices" which will help us to better resist his attacks.

If what you read here helps you to appreciate more fully the reality of the conflict between Christ and Satan, if it helps you to understand more fully the part each of us plays in that conflict, and if this understanding helps you to fortify your resistance to the enemy, then all of us who have had a part in the experience related here will be happy and grateful.

One

"I won't let her pray. I won't let her pray. I won't let her sleep. I won't let her sleep. And I am going to kill her!"

These were the first words the demon spoke to us, a refrain that I heard repeated quite often during the next few weeks.

When I first heard these words, Paula Green was lying on her bed in our trailer parked in our driveway. Her eyes were closed; and except for the movement of her lips, she appeared to be asleep. But the voice, loud and coarse, was not Paula's.

My wife and I were surprised but not shocked. Some things Paula had said and done during the previous few weeks had raised questions in our minds. And now the voice we heard and the words it spoke confirmed what we had already come to suspect. *Paula was possessed by a demon.*

Later that evening my mind went back to the telephone call I had received some eight months earlier from my friend, Dr. Smith.

"Pastor, would you have time during the next day or so to call on one of my patients who is in the hospital? She is recuperating from a concussion she received from a fall during a hike in the mountains. She is interested in talking to one of our ministers."

"Of course I'll see her. I'll try to get over there this afternoon or tomorrow."

And that is how I first met Paula Green. She was a young lady in her late twenties who had come as a patient to the doctor's office a few months earlier. Because of her previous work experience in medical offices and because he needed help at the time, Dr. Smith employed her in his office. She had worked only about two months, however, when the hiking accident occurred. During that short time Dr. and Mrs. Smith had interested her in the study of the Bible. They had also taken her to the first of a series of meetings being conducted in a neighboring city by Pastor William Fagal of the "Faith for Today" telecast. She had been so intrigued by what she learned that she had returned every night. All this I learned during my first visit with Paula in the hospital that day in October.

Paula was discharged from the hospital a day or two after my first visit, and my wife and I arranged to study the Bible with her in her apartment every Tuesday evening.

In January came the first in a series of events that was to change her life much more than any of us realized at the time. At first it did not seem too unusual. Paula simply began to experience a feeling of general physical weakness.

"I must be coming down with the flu," she said one Tuesday evening. "I just don't have any strength. Sometimes I don't think I can make it through the day. And when I get home, I can hardly get up the stairs to my apartment."

We assumed that Paula would soon regain her strength, but instead she gradually grew weaker. Eventually she had to spend some time in a hospital just to be built up physically. After a short period of rest at home she tried to resume her duties in Dr. Smith's office, but she was just not strong enough.

While Paula was in the hospital, Dr. Smith kept her on his payroll, a generosity which she appreciated. But when she realized she was not going to be able to perform her duties after her discharge from the hospital, she asked that her employment be terminated. Left without income, she became deeply concerned about her future. My wife and I assured her that our heavenly Father knew her needs, that He had a plan for her life, and that He would provide for her needs in His own way and in His own time.

The telephone rang a few days later while Paula was in our home visiting with my wife. Did Mrs. Allen know of a lady who would be interested in "living in" with a physically handicapped woman? The work would not be hard, but it would require being in the home twenty-four hours a day, with weekends off.

"Yes," my wife replied. "I believe I know just the person you want." She called Paula to the telephone.

As a result of this conversation and the interview that followed, Paula was employed as the nurse-companion to Mrs. Miller, whose daughter had called. It was agreed that Paula would begin her duties three weeks later. In the meantime she flew east to visit her relatives, including her two young children living in foster homes.

When she returned from her trip east, Paula was enjoying better health than she had for several months. This fact made her confident that she would be able to do the work her new job required. She was sure that her new job was a direct answer to her prayers and ours. She appeared especially happy when she was baptized on the Sabbath after she returned from the East. Her future looked bright; Paula was encouraged.

However, this hopeful outlook for the future changed in a matter of days. While her new work was not hard physically, it was more demanding in other ways than anticipated. Mrs. Miller's condition was such that Paula had to give her considerable attention during the day besides doing the routine household duties. And during the night there were many occasions when Mrs. Miller needed attention. Paula had been on her new job only about a week when she found sleep increasingly difficult. On many nights, even when Mrs. Miller did not require attention, she got almost no sleep.

As Mrs. Allen and I continued our Tuesday evening Bible studies with Paula, we could not help seeing the changes coming over her. She looked extremely tired. Eyes dull, she complained of headaches. When she told us of her inability to sleep, we assured her that in a little while she would adjust to the routine and that if she would only be patient things would "work out."

Things "worked out," but not in the way we had expected. We noticed that Paula's arms and legs were covered with red spots that appeared to be bruises. She said similar marks were on other parts of her body. She told us she did not know what caused them. She guessed she just "bruised easily."

Paula did not have the use of a car at this time, and one day she called and asked if I could take her to an appointment with her personal physician. She arranged for a neighbor lady to stay with Mrs. Miller for a couple of hours while she was away. When Paula came out of the doctor's office, she was almost in a state of shock.

"He wants to put me in the hospital right now," she told me. "He doesn't even want me to go home to get my things."

But she explained to the doctor that the lady who was relieving her at Mrs. Miller's could stay only for an hour or so and that other arrangements must be made before she could enter the hospital. On the way back to Mrs. Miller's we stopped and picked up a young lady I knew who said she could substitute for Paula for a day or so until other plans could be made. Then Paula put a few things in an overnight bag, and I took her back to the hospital, where she was admitted. We learned later that she was suffering from "extreme fatigue," according to her chart. It was then the last of April, and Paula was back where she had been in January, in spite of our high hopes for her future and our belief that her job was an answer to prayer.

Again, as in January, it took about two weeks for Paula to be built up from her physical weakness. The hospital is only three blocks from my home; and because I felt that Paula needed all the support she could get, I visited her every day.

During one of my visits with Paula, just before she left the hospital, she made a remark whose significance I failed to appreciate at the time. "Pastor Allen," she said, "I feel as though there is a devil in me."

"You know that isn't true," I replied. "You have recently been baptized. You are one of God's children. You can't have a devil in you."

Six weeks later I learned how wrong I was.

Two

When Paula was admitted to the hospital the last part of April, her doctor told her she must not return to her former work if she valued her health. This left her again without employment. After her discharge from the hospital two weeks later, finding a place to live became a very real problem. So, at our invitation, she came to live with us. Our daughter and her children were visiting us for the summer, and all our bedrooms were occupied. But Paula was able to move into our travel trailer parked at the end of our driveway.

Even while Paula was still in the hospital, we prayed about her future. Her need of employment was so acute that she was prepared to accept almost any kind of work, anywhere. We prayed that God would lead in this matter and open and close doors according to His wisdom and will. So when the opportunity came for her to go to work at a nearby hospital, she was very happy. She felt, as my wife and I did, that this was a definite answer to prayer.

But only a couple of weeks had passed before it became apparent that already something was wrong and Paula's health again was beginning to deteriorate. Her headaches returned. She complained of feeling weak. She was so drowsy during the day that she could hardly stay awake, but she could not sleep at night. At times she expressed to me feelings of guilt and worthlessness. Nothing I could say or do appeared to have any lasting effect.

"Why don't you give up on me?" she would ask. "Just forget about me and leave me alone. Let me go my way, and I won't be a burden on you any longer."

We would assure her that she was not a burden, that God had not given up and neither had we.

"Just don't give up on me," she pleaded at other times. "No matter what I say or do, don't give up on me."

Again we would assure her that we were not about to give up, that God loved her and had a plan for her life. Then I would share with her some Bible promises, and we would pray.

One of the promises we shared most often during this period is found in Psalm 37:3-5. "Trust in the Lord, and do good; so shalt thou dwell in the land, and verily thou shalt be fed. Delight thyself also in the Lord; and he shall give thee the desires of thine heart. Commit thy way unto the Lord; trust also in him, and he shall bring it to pass."

But as time passed, it was becoming increasingly difficult for Paula to pray or to study her Bible as she had enjoyed doing only a few weeks before.

Paula was experiencing noticeable personality changes too. She was sensitive, irritable, easily offended, and moody. During the last few weeks before "things broke open," she was like a time bomb. We never knew when she was going to explode.

I know that some of Paula's problems are commonly associated with a condition which we generally classify as "depression." I also understand that a lack of certain vitamins in the diet can result in several of the symptoms Paula had. But during this time Paula did and said some strange things that seemed to indicate something more. Some of these things were of a personal nature and need not be recorded here. It was at these times that she would say, "No matter what I do or say, don't give up on me."

About the time Paula was baptized, she met Donna at a Friday-evening Bible study conducted by Pastor Paddock. The two young women became good friends the first time they met.

While Paula was staying with us after she came home from the hospital, Donna invited her to stay in her home while Donna was away on vacation. During the ten days or so that Paula lived in Donna's home, we naturally had less communication with her than we had before, and we were not entirely aware of what was going on.

Then at 1:30 on a Thursday morning I was awakened by the telephone's ringing. It was Paula. Her speech was so slurred I could hardly recognize her voice.

"Please come and help me. I can't find my car keys. And something is wrong with me. I don't know why I did it, but I ran out into the street, and I fell down and hurt my knees and elbows. And I—"

"Stay right where you are," I interrupted. "We will be right over. Be calm and pray, Paula, and everything will be all right."

I woke my wife, we dressed quickly, and I drove across town as fast as I dared. When Paula opened the door in response to my knock, her eyes were glazed. She said she had a headache and double vision. She staggered drunkenly when she walked. Her arms and hands appeared rigid and moved mechanically. When we asked whether she had taken a drug, she vehemently denied it.

We helped her out of the house and into our car.

When we arrived at our home, we had to help her out of the car and into our house. My wife applied medicine to her bruised knees and elbows. Then Paula said she was hungry, and she asked if she could have a bowl of breakfast cereal. After she had eaten, we helped her into the trailer, and my wife helped her prepare for bed.

We hoped, of course, that Paula's problems would have disappeared when she woke up later in the morning. But she still complained of having a headache and double vision. Her speech was slurred; and her movements, although they were less mechanical than they had been earlier, were still not normal. It was obvious that something was still wrong.

She chose to stay in the trailer rather than to come into the house. But in the middle of the morning, while my wife was having a Bible study with a lady who came to our home regularly for that purpose, Paula literally staggered into the house. She fell before she reached the room where my wife was, and crawled the rest of the way on her hands and knees, making a pitiable sight and a shock for my wife and her Bible student.

"I guess I'm worse than I realized," Paula gasped. "I need to go to the emergency room. Where is Pastor Allen?"

I was not at home, and so the Bible student volunteered to take her to the hospital.

When I came home a little later and learned what had happened, I went immediately to the emergency room and found Paula still undergoing tests. I must admit that I was surprised when blood tests revealed no evidence of the presence of drugs.

Paula was in the hospital one week. During that time most of her problems disappeared. Her physical movements became normal and her speech only slightly slurred. But the severe headache continued. The tests

17

that were administered, including a brain scan and spinal puncture, revealed no cause of the headache.

"She still complains of a severe headache," her doctor told me. "We've given her all the tests we can. I don't doubt her having the headache, but we can find no reason for it."

Dr. Smith called me during the week Paula was in the hospital. We naturally talked about Paula's problem. We observed that three times during the past few months the bottom had dropped out of her plans just when things seemed to be going well. It had happened when she was working in Dr. Smith's office. It had happened soon after she began to work for Mrs. Miller. And now it had happened again, just a few days after she had begun her work at the hospital. Illness, with its resulting change of plans, can happen to anyone and probably has happened to many of us at some time in our lives. But there seemed to be something uncanny about its happening so often to the same person in so short a time and without any detectable medical reason.

"Pastor," the doctor asked, "have you ever considered the possibility of there being supernatural forces at work in Paula's life?"

Immediately my mind went back to the remark Paula had made to me when she had been in the hospital three months before: "I feel as though there is a devil in me." I determined right then to talk with her further about the matter at the first opportunity. I shared my thinking with Dr. Smith and told him about the remark Paula had made.

"By the way," Dr. Smith asked, "have you heard the tape by Elder Gardner?" Elder Gardner's parish was several hundred miles from our home.

"No," I replied, "I've never heard the tape. I've never even heard about it."

The doctor then explained that the tape related the experience of the pastor's wife, who apparently had some of the same physical and emotional problems that Paula had. The tape, Dr. Smith continued, told how several demons had been cast out of her and how God had apparently given her victory over the powers that had controlled her.

"Would you like to have a copy of the tape?" Dr. Smith asked.

"Yes, I certainly would," I replied.

"Then I'll bring you a copy in a day or so."

True to his word, Dr. Smith brought me a copy of the tape the next evening, and I listened to it the following day.

I believe now that the tape's coming into my possession just when it did was providential, for it provided me with insights and procedures that were invaluable to me a few days later, when I dealt with a situation similar to that of the pastor's wife.

Wednesday afternoon, after I had listened to the tape, I visited Paula again in the hospital.

"Do you remember telling me several weeks ago that you felt as though there was a devil in you?" I asked her.

"Oh, yes," she answered. "And I still feel that way. There *is* a devil in me, and he has been there a long time." The assertive way in which she made the statement strengthened my intention of talking further with her about it.

"I don't think this is the time or the place to talk about it," I told her; "but when you come home, I want to discuss this matter some more."

Two days later, on Friday, June 30, Paula called from the hospital.

"Can you come and get me? They are going to let me

go home today. I still have the headache, but the doctor says I might as well be home as here. He says for me to stay in bed most of the time and to be quiet, and he thinks that in a few days the headache will go away."

"Let me know when you want to talk about your feeling about the devil," I reminded her on the way home. "I want to talk with you only when you feel the time is right."

Paula did not wait long. Late that same day she sent word by one of our grandchildren that she wanted to talk to Mrs. Allen and me privately in the trailer. So about sundown we went to the trailer to talk with her. In harmony with the doctor's instructions, she was lying down; but when we entered the trailer, she sat up and came immediately to the point.

"Do you see this little chain on my ankle?" she asked.

"Yes, I've noticed it. I planned to talk with you about it, but there hasn't seemed to be an appropriate time."

"Mike gave it to me," she explained. "When he gave it to me, he said that he and that chain would control me the rest of my life. But now I am afraid of it. Do you think it would be all right if I took it off?"

"Not only would it be all right, you *should.*" I knew that Mike was a non-Christian friend of Paula's. Without saying another word, she reached down, gave the chain a slight tug, and handed it to me. I felt that this was Paula's way of telling me she wanted to talk, her way of asking for help.

"Perhaps this is a good time for us to talk about what you said in the hospital about the devil," I suggested.

"Yes. He is still there."

Some months before this, I had obtained a copy of "Warfare Prayer." This rather lengthy prayer expresses a total commitment to God and a definite stand against the devil and all his works. Anticipating that I might need them, I took two copies of the prayer with me when my wife and I went to the trailer to talk with Paula.

After Paula indicated a desire to talk, I explained to her that God could cast the demon out of her only if she made a full commitment to God.

"This is not a game," I told her. "It is a matter of life and death. Your eternal life is at stake. If you expect God to deliver you from the demon that you say is in you, you must make a thorough commitment to God. That commitment must be so definite that both God and the devil know exactly where you stand."

Then I gave Paula a copy of "Warfare Prayer."

"This prayer is not a magic formula," I explained. "It has meaning only as it expresses your personal conviction about Christ and Satan and your relationship to each of them. If this prayer does not express your commitment to Jesus Christ as your personal Saviour and your individual rejection of Satan and all his work, it is for you only so many meaningless words on paper.

As Paula read the prayer, my wife and I prayed silently.

When she had finished, Paula said, "This is exactly the way I feel."

"Then I want you to read it out loud as your personal prayer to God for deliverance from the demon that is in you. Mrs. Allen and I will be praying too."

Paula sat up on her bed. My wife and I knelt beside her and read the prayer silently as she read it aloud.

"Heavenly Father, I bow in worship and praise before you. I cover myself with the blood of the Lord Jesus Christ as my protection during this time of prayer. I surrender myself completely and unreservedly in every area of my life to Yourself."

Then she paused, so long that I looked up. She was staring at the paper, apparently trying to read; but no words came.

"I can't read it," she said.

"Yes, you can." I tried to encourage her. "Just read the next sentence."

"I can't." Then she fell back on her pillow. Her voice became loud and coarse. "I won't let her pray! I won't let her pray! I won't let her sleep! I won't let her sleep! And I am going to kill her!"

Paula was now stretched out full length on the bed. Her eyes were closed, and she appeared to be asleep. While she remained in this condition, I read the next sentence of the prayer, the one she could not read. "I do take a stand against all the workings of Satan that would hinder me in this time of prayer, and I address myself only to the true and living God and refuse any involvement with Satan with my prayer." Then I continued to read the prayer as my wife and I knelt beside Paula's bed. But whenever the pronoun *I* occurred, I substituted Paula's name.

Paula appeared to be asleep as I read the prayer, but as soon as I had finished and said Amen, she opened her eyes, rubbing them as though she were waking from a nap.

"What happened?" she asked. She said she could remember nothing that happened from the time she first began to read until she "woke up." We later found this lack of memory or lapse of time to be characteristic of each encounter with the demons. No matter what she said or did while the demon was in control, she had no later recollection. We discovered, too, that these blank spots in her memory sometimes began a few minutes before the encounter and sometimes extended briefly beyond, until she woke up.

At the time of this first encounter, after Paula woke up, I explained what had happened. She did not seem alarmed as I thought she might be, but she accepted the information almost as a matter of fact. Some weeks later, after God had given her victory over the demons, she told me she was convinced that once we had got into the matter, we would "open up a whole new can of worms."

Again I wanted to be sure that Paula realized how serious the situation really was.

"We know for sure now that we are not playing games. This is for real, Paula. You must understand that your eternal life is now at stake. You and all of us must stay close to Jesus. We must pray as we have never prayed before."

She said she understood. In spite of the demon's statement that he would not let her pray, Paula offered a prayer of dedication and commitment. Since we thought she might be apprehensive, Mrs. Allen offered to sleep in the trailer with her that night. But she declined, saying she would be all right.

When she came into the house the next morning, she was more relaxed and cheerful than she had been for many weeks. Because of the slight headache which still persisted and because of the doctor's order to be quiet, she did not plan to go to church. After breakfast she lay down on the davenport and listened to the church music and the church service on a local radio station. She was still listening when we came home.

"This is the best Sabbath I can remember," she said. "The church service was good, and the music is beautiful. And I feel so relaxed."

Later I remarked to my wife how different Paula was from what she had been the last few weeks. We both expressed the hope that this was the beginning of a new experience that would continue.

But our hopes were short-lived. In the middle of the afternoon, while Mrs. Allen and I were reading in the living room, Paula came in from the trailer and asked abruptly, "Do you suppose I could cook some cauliflower and broccoli?"

We knew that these were two of her favorite vegetables, and we made it a point to have them on hand. She knew there were some in the refrigerator. But her request took us by surprise.

"You know this is Sabbath, Paula," my wife said. "And we don't do any cooking like that in our home on Sabbath. If you are hungry, I will get you something light to eat. Or we can fix the vegetables later, after sundown. But we won't cook them on Sabbath."

At this, Paula became very indignant. She said some extremely caustic things about the Sabbath and slammed the door as she went to the trailer, where she stayed the rest of the afternoon.

Early in the evening she came back into the house and sat down at the table where I was reading.

"I am not going to your church any more," she announced. "I'm going to my aunt's church. It's easier. She doesn't have to worry about the Sabbath." With that, she got up and left.

This experience about the Sabbath was very much like one we had had several weeks earlier, before Paula went to the hospital. She had come into the living room and announced, "I'm going to the store to buy some shampoo. Is there anything I can get for you?"

For a fraction of a second I thought Paula must have forgotten what day it was. "Paula," I said, "this is Sabbath. You know we don't buy anything on Sabbath unless it's a real emergency—a need to buy something like medicine. Wait until after Sabbath. Please."

She did not say anything in reply, but soon she went back to the trailer, where, so far as I knew, she stayed until the next morning.

Hatred of the true Sabbath has been one of the common factors in each of the several cases of demon possession with which I have been involved. And in each instance this hatred of the Sabbath has been accompanied by a hatred of God's Word. Destruction of the Bible or attempts to destroy the Bible seem to be common in demon possession.

The day after Paula became upset at not being able to cook the vegetables, she put a few of her things in her car and went to spend a few days at Donna's home again. So during the next few days we had very little communication with her. Hopefully, she was resting, getting rid of her headache and in general getting back in shape so she could return to her work at the hospital.

And then about six o'clock on a Tuesday morning she appeared unexpectedly at our door.

"I need help," she announced. "But this time it isn't for me. It's for Donna. She and Bert had an argument, and Donna lost control of herself. She sort of went berserk. It lasted so long that I finally took her to the emergency room. But they did not have a bed available for a female patient in the mental health unit. Donna refused to go back to her home, and so we have been in a motel all night. It's been a real nightmare. She keeps threatening to take her life. I've taken shears, razor blades, and knives away from her. I just can't take any more of this, or I'll be back in the hospital myself. I can't afford that. I've got to go back to work, or I'll lose my job. You've got to come and help."

Paula left then to go back to the motel while I dressed. Under the pressure of the situation Paula had neglected to tell me specifically what motel she and Donna were staying in, and I forgot to ask. Consequently it took me some time to locate the right place. When I did arrive at the correct motel about an hour later, I found the two women and Pastor Paddock, whom Paula had called on the telephone. He left to meet another appointment soon after I arrived. When I called the hospital, I was told that there would probably be no bed available for Donna until the next day at the earliest. This meant she would have to spend another night at the motel because she still refused to return to her home, and I felt that to force her to do so against her will might aggravate her emotional problem.

It was evident that Paula badly needed physical and emotional rest, and so I arranged for her to occupy another room at the motel. Then I called one of the women of the church, who agreed to stay with Donna that night. A telephone call from the hospital the next day informed me that there was a bed for Donna if I would take her to the emergency room immediately. Of course I did.

In the meantime Paula stayed in her room and tried to get some rest. Her experience with Donna had left her physically and emotionally drained. But sleep came only occasionally. During this time we communicated with her each morning by telephone, with the understanding that she would initiate the calls so that we would not disturb her if she was sleeping. Mrs. Allen prepared meals which we took to her two or three times each day, depending upon her wishes. We continued to do this during the two weeks Paula was in the motel.

Three

Paula's experience entered a new phase on Friday, July 14. She called me late in the morning, when I was at the church.

"Pastor Allen, come and help me—quick! The devil is after me. He is putting terrible thoughts in my mind, and I can't get them out."

"Pray, Paula, pray. Pray and claim God's promises in the name of Jesus. I'll be there right away."

I called Pastor Doyle's home, but no one responded. So I got into my car and headed for Paula's motel room. In fear of what might happen because of the demon's previous threat to kill her, I am sure I broke the speed limit, hoping to arrive there in time to prevent a tragedy.

She unlocked and opened the door. But it was not the Paula we knew. Her eyes were glazed; and when she spoke, it was not her voice but the same demon voice I had heard earlier, in the trailer.

"Who are you?" the voice asked.

"I am a minister of the gospel of the Lord Jesus Christ, and in His name I demand that you tell me who you are."

"I am Satan. Why are you here?"

"I am here to ask God to help Paula, and I'm glad I'm here."

"Don't say that name! I hate that name!"

At first I thought that the outburst was directed against my use of God's name. But for some reason which my friends and I never learned the objection was to using Paula's name. Later we learned to refer to her as "this girl," "this person," "the girl you are controlling." If from habit or by a slip of the tongue we did use her name, the demon always objected.

After objecting to my use of Paula's name, the demon repeated what he had said the first time we heard his voice: "I won't let her pray, I won't let her sleep, and I am going to kill her." This became a refrain that I was to hear repeated many times during the next few days. Sometimes the voice added, "And I am going to make her lose her job."

During this brief conversation Paula had lain down on her bed. I did the only thing I knew to do under the circumstances. I prayed. I prayed, as I did at each of the succeeding encounters, that the demons would not be permitted to injure Paula in any way. And God answered my prayer, as He did in all these encounters. She relaxed and seemed to fall into a natural sleep. In all this experience covering the next two weeks and involving some eighteen or twenty encounters, the demons were never permitted to injure her in any way although there were repeated threats and several attempts to do so.

I prayed that God would not permit the devil to speak and that He would give Paula rest. For some reason which I cannot explain, I did not at that time ask God to deliver her from the demon.

While Paula slept, I called Dr. Smith from her bedside phone. I told him briefly what had happened, and we agreed that we must surely be dealing with supernatural forces. He suggested that I come to his home, where he could discuss the events further. I told him I would be there as soon as I could leave Paula.

When I had completed the telephone conversation, I knelt by Paula's bed and prayed again. When I finished, Paula woke up, just as she had at the end of the "Warfare Prayer." But she could remember nothing after her call to me. This was true in each of the future encounters. She could always remember calling me on the phone, but nothing after that until she woke up. It seemed that the demon took control of her mind after she called, blanking out her memory.

After Paula woke up that Friday, we talked again about the necessity of her making a complete commitment to God. We read from the Bible, I prayed, and again—in spite of the demon's statement that he would not let Paula pray—she offered a beautiful prayer for deliverance. Then she assured me that she felt all right and that she was not afraid. So I left her in order to keep my appointment with Dr. Smith.

He and I spent more than an hour together, reviewing the events of the past two weeks. Then he called Elder R. Allen Anderson. We knew that he had had some experience in dealing with demon possession, and I felt the need of his counsel. Elder Anderson invited me to come to his home immediately.

I spent another two hours with him, discussing in detail all I knew about Paula's case. He said that, based on the information I had given him, he had no doubt that at times Paula was being controlled by a demon. We agreed that Elder Anderson, Pastor Doyle, Paula, and I would meet at the church the next Sunday afternoon.

That night passed without incident. The next day was Sabbath. I asked the members of our congregation to pray especially for a young lady who was facing a severe crisis in her life, without mentioning her by name or citing details. Paula was still living in the motel and did not go to church that day. We invited her to come to our home for Sabbath dinner, and she said she would come on condition that we would understand if she left and went back to her room right after dinner. We assured her that we would understand.

Paula arrived at our home soon after we came home from church. We could see that things were not entirely right. Her eyes were noticeably dull, and her physical coordination was poor. Although she complained of a headache, she seemed to enjoy the meal; and she carried on a normal conversation. But she excused herself almost immediately after finishing the meal, saying that she wanted to get back to her room "before something happened." But the afternoon and night passed uneventfully.

Sunday afternoon I had not yet told Paula about our proposed meeting at the church. About three o'clock, while I was working at the church and wondering how best to get Paula's cooperation, the telephone rang. It was Paula.

"Pastor Allen, I need your help again. I've written awful things about God on the mirror in my room. I didn't want to do it, but I could not help it." At that point the voice became loud and coarse.

"Is that you again? Why are you interfering with my work? Everything was fine until you came along. This girl was doing what I wanted her to do. Now you have brought the battle out into the open. I am going to kill her."

"Who are you?" I asked.

"I don't have to tell you my name; I don't have to tell you anything."

"Yes, you do. The Lord Jesus Christ has already overcome you at the cross, and in His name I demand that you tell me who you are."

"I am Lucifer, the light of the world."

"No, you are not Lucifer. You lost that position when you rebelled in heaven. You are now Satan. Jesus Christ is the Light of the World, and in His name I demand that you tell me the truth. Who are you?"

"I am the devil. I am not going to let her pray. I am not going to let her sleep. I am going to kill her. But I don't have to talk with you. I am going to hang up."

Down went the receiver, and all I could hear was the dial tone.

It was just at that time that Elder Anderson arrived at the church to keep our appointmnt. I told him Paula was in trouble. I was going to her room to get her. I would be right back. I do not know why it did not occur to me to ask him to go with me. On the way to Paula's room I prayed that God would not allow her to be hurt in any way and that He would permit us to get back to the church safely.

As I look back on this entire experience, I am impressed with the way God worked for us and answered our prayers in small but very important ways. God saw to it that I was always available when Paula needed me. Never did she call without being able to reach me either at home or at the church. And in every case she was able to express her need before the demon took control of her voice. And He always saw to it that Paula opened her door, which she kept locked, in response to my knock. Each time the need arose—and there were many—I prayed that God would not allow the demon to keep her from opening the door. And every time, with only one exception, Paula opened the door. God also always saw to it that I remembered to pick up the key to Paula's motel room before I left, so I could get back into the room. This might seem trivial, but under the pressure of the situation, it would have been very easy for me to forget. God never permitted this, and I am very thankful.

When Paula came to the door that Sunday afternoon, she was not as fully under demon control as she had been when she called or as she was to become before the afternoon's experience ended. But it was obvious that she had been in trouble earlier.

"See what I wrote on the mirror" she said, leading me to the dressing room. "I did not want to do it, but I could not help it."

Written on the mirror with material from Paula's makeup kit were filthy words and expressions. And each expression contained some name pertaining to the Deity. Using bathroom tissue, I wiped the words from the mirror as fast as I could, but it took longer than I expected it would. As I worked, I explained to Paula that we were going to go to the church, where we could talk and pray. She did not object when I suggested a little later that she get into my car.

There was very little conversation during the fifteen-minute ride to the church. I did not want to cause any difficulty while driving, but I talked much with God during that trip and during the others that followed.

By the time we arrived at the church, Paula seemed to be in control of herself. Pastor Doyle was there as we had planned. After I introduced Paula to Elder Anderson, we gave our full attention to the purpose for which we had met. We prayed, and we spent considerable time talking with Paula about the importance of her making a complete commitment to God, without any reservation whatsoever. And when we knelt to pray later, Paula offered a prayer of confession and commitment. All of us prayed that God would give her complete victory over the powers that sought to control her.

However, she did not gain the victory that afternoon. She later admitted that there were sins in her life that she was cherishing and which she was not at that time willing to give up. We felt that afternoon that this was the case, because the demon took over again before we left the room.

She walked around the room most of the time, talking in the loud, coarse voice that I had learned to recognize. Most of what she said was uncomplimentary to God, and many of her expressions were a repetition of what she had written on the mirror earlier that afternoon. During this time we three ministers prayed. We prayed again that Paula would not be allowed to injure herself, that the Holy Spirit would penetrate her demon-clouded mind so that she could make everything right with God and that He could thus give her complete victory.

Eventually the voice said, "I am going to leave." Paula went down the steps leading from the church office to the rear door. We learned from this experience to lock all doors behind us. Fortunately, the outside door was locked; and while she fumbled with the lock, I caught up with her and prevented her from opening the door. There at the foot of the steps we three ministers again prayed that the Holy Spirit would beat back the powers of darkness and give her the desire and ability to make a complete commitment to God. While we were praying, Paula fainted, bumped her head on the wall, and slumped to the floor. We pulled her away from the wall to a more comfortable position and continued to pray.

In a few minutes she woke up and went with us up the steps and back into the church office. There we prayed again, but it was not long before the demon took over and began to speak in the loud voice. Paula walked over

33

to a floral piece on a table, took one of the flowers and slowly, deliberately tore it into pieces—petal by petal, leaf by leaf. Again the voice spoke. ''My work is to kill and destroy.''

Suddenly Paula again slumped to the floor and fell into a kind of sleep. We picked up the torn bits of flower and continued to pray. In a short time she woke up, apparently in full control of her faculties.

Again she said she could remember nothing of what had happened from the time she called me on the phone until she woke up there in the church office. Everything that had happened between these two events was seemingly erased. We explained briefly what had happened, had another season of prayer, and I took Paula back to her room. That night passed without further incident.

Although we had earnestly prayed and claimed God's promise of victory, we had as yet been given no evidence of victory. The demon's presence had been manifest in the destruction of the flower and in his voice almost to the time we left the church. We could account for the lack of victory over the demon power only by assuming that Paula was holding something back from God, cherishing some sin. How else could one explain the failure of deliverance? We know that it is not God's will that any of His children be controlled by demons. So we did not pray, ''Deliver this girl from this power, *if it is your will*.'' And God, who has already won the victory at the cross, is stronger than all the demons combined. So we did not pray, ''Deliver this girl from demon control *if it is possible*.'' Willfully cherished sin is the only barrier to victory over demon possession. Paula later confessed that this was so in her case.

Monday morning passed without incident. About three o'clock in the aftrnoon I drove home from my office for a short break before beginning the evening's duties. My oldest daughter met me at the door, an expression of distress on her face.

"Go to Paula's! Go to Paula's quick!" she shouted. "Paula just called. She needs help badly."

By that time my wife and young daughter were also at the door.

"Phone Elder Anderson and ask him to meet me at Paula's room just as soon as he can get there. And keep praying. And you'd better come with me," I called to my older daughter.

I always felt that it was very important to get to Paula as soon as possible whenever she called for help. The demon's threat "I am going to kill her" stayed in my mind.

Elder Anderson responded to Mrs. Allen's telephone call and quickly agreed to join us. I believe God saw to that too.

I drove as fast as I dared to Paula's motel, went to her room, and knocked. She did not answer. After repeatedly knocking and calling, I went to the manager for a key. He went to the room with me and opened the door.

Paula was nowhere in sight. On her bed was the motel's Gideon Bible. But it no longer resembled a Bible. It had been torn into little pieces as though it had been run through a paper shredder, and it was scattered all over the bed.

"Paula! Paula! Paula!"

No answer.

I walked around to the far side of the bed and saw her lying on the floor, unconscious.

Taking in the scene, the motel manager said, "Come and see me before you leave." Then he closed the door and went back to his office.

My daughter and I knelt beside Paula and prayed. We

prayed again that Paula would not be harmed or injured and would wake up soon. We pleaded that somehow the Holy Spirit would impress her to make a full confession and forsake any cherished sin so that God could give her complete victory over her tormentor.

Elder Anderson arrived while we were praying.

"Dear Lord," I prayed, "send your Holy Spirit to penetrate the fog with which Satan has filled Paula's mind. If it is Your will, enable us to communicate with her just now as we speak to her."

Then I said softly, "Paula, if you can hear me, nod your head."

She nodded her head slightly.

"Now, if you can still hear me, say 'Jesus.' "

"Jesus," came faintly but audibly.

"Now, say 'help.' "

"Help." Paula's voice, still a whisper, was a little more audible.

"Say 'me.' "

"Me." Her voice was definitely stronger.

"Now," I said, "say all three words as a prayer. 'Jesus, help me.' "

"Jesus—help—me," she said in a voice almost normal.

She opened her eyes and woke up.

In each of the eighteen or twenty encounters that followed during the next few days, I followed the same procedure. In every case, God answered my prayer and caused Paula to wake up. And after the first time or two she always woke up with a smile.

We cleaned up the debris of the shredded Bible before Paula woke up; so she never saw the results of the destruction Satan caused her to do. However, she is aware of what happened. She had told Mrs. Allen when she called for help on the phone that she was tearing up the Bible although she did not want to do it.

Each encounter was debilitating emotionally and physically to all of us, especially to Paula. After Monday's experience, she lay on the bed, just resting. Soon she said she was hungry, and my daughter went in my car to a drive-in to get her something to eat. She had eaten only a little, however, when she excused herself to go the bathroom. When she came out of the bathroom, we saw the change.

Her eyes were glazed, her speech slurred. On her way back to her bed she saw a table fork lying on the shelf. Before I could stop her she grabbed it and attempted to stab her left wrist, but I was able to take it from her before she injured herself.

It seemed wise at this point to get Paula out of the motel. I knew from previous experience that the demons would probably yell loudly during these encounters, and we did not want to attract attention to what was happening or to place ourselves in a situation where we could be accused of disturbing the peace.

Neither did we want to earn the ill will of the motel manager, who was already puzzled about what he had seen in Paula's room. He had already asked us to see him before we left. I knew he would expect some explanation of what he had seen, but I was not sure how much I should tell him. Elder Anderson and I went to his office.

We told him that Paula had an "emotional problem" and that she had experienced an "incident." We told him we were ministers who were working with her and that we were confident everything would be all right. He said he was anxious to protect the reputation of the motel and to see that no damage was done to the property. He cautioned us that the occupant would be held responsible financially for any damage. I suspect he thought Paula was on drugs. But he did not ask that she move, and we were thankful.

When we finished talking with the manager, I asked Paula to get into the car to go to the church; and she cooperated.

Four

We took Paula to the church, as I have explained, in order to have more privacy than the motel could provide, and to avoid the possibility of attracting attention or disturbing the peace. Paula was under demon control. I prayed without ceasing for God's protection, for both Paula and myself. I intentionally limited our conversation because I wanted to avoid saying anything that would excite either Paula or the demons who spoke through her.

In spite of this, there were times when I had to ask God to limit the demons' speaking.

A theme the demons repeated on several trips from the motel to the church went like this:

"I hate you. You are interfering. Things were going well until you came along. Now every time I open my eyes, you are there. You have brought the battle out in the open. Now I have to kill her."

In one case we had thought that a certain demon had been cast out, only to learn at the next encounter that he was still there. On the way to the church that time the demon said, "You thought I was gone, didn't you? I almost fooled you, didn't I? That's all right. I almost fooled myself." I still don't know what he meant by that last remark.

Elder Anderson, who had left his car at the motel, rode with Paula and me to the church. When we arrived, I called Pastor Doyle, who joined us a few minutes later.

Beginning Monday afternoon, the encounters, or confrontations, with few exceptions, were intentionally induced; and we followed the same procedures each time. We always asked Paula to lie on the floor with a pillow under her head. This she did without objecting. The prone position made it easier to restrain her and to keep her from injuring herself. And the pillow prevented one of the demons' favorite tricks—to hurt her by bumping her head up and down against the floor.

After these safety measures had been taken we always prayed. We prayed first that God would banish from Paula's body and mind and from the room and the entire building all demons who were not directly involved in tormenting or controlling her. Then we prayed that those demons who remained would not be permitted to injure her in any way. We prayed for the forgiveness of our sins and for a relationship to Jesus Christ that would permit Him to use us in any way He saw fit. We prayed for a greater measure of faith to believe that God could and would give Paula the victory over the demons that controlled her. Last, we prayed that God would send the Holy Spirit into Paula's body and mind in full measure, that the Holy Spirit would do battle with the demons that were present, and that this battle would result in complete victory.

When we finished praying, we read Matthew 10:1, 5-8. "And when he had called unto him his twelve disciples, *he gave them power against unclean spirits, to cast them out,* and to heal all manner of sickness and all manner of disease. . . . These twelve Jesus sent forth, and commanded, saying, Go not unto the Gentiles, and into any city of the Samaritans enter ye not. But go rather to the lost sheep of the house of Israel. And as ye go preach, saying, The kingdom of heaven is at hand. Heal the sick, cleanse the lepers, raise the dead, cast out devils: freely ye have received, freely give."

When the words "cast out devils" were read, Paula's arms and legs would begin to move and twitch. Then in a matter of seconds her entire body would thrash about so violently that it would require three or four of us to restrain her. Her body responded in this manner to the words "cast out devils" at each reading, without exception, as long as any demons remained.

As soon as the physical action began, indicating the presence of a demon, I would demand in the name of the Lord Jesus Christ that the demon identify himself.

"In the name of Jesus Christ, who shed His blood for Paula's sins, I demand that you identify yourself. What is your name?"

Hesitation. Then came the reply, "I don't have to tell you my name."

"Yes, you must tell me your name because I demand it in the name of Jesus Christ, who at the cross has already won the victory over all demons."

God always caused the demons to obey. Eight different demons identified themselves that Monday afternoon. That day was the beginning of the victory which came three days later. Each of the eight demons identified himself by the name of some person who had played a part in Paula's life. (These are people who are living persons, whom Paula knows, and for this reason I have employed fictitious names in this account.)

"I demand in the name of Jesus Christ," I went on, "that you tell us your assignment in controlling this girl."

Again came the horrible voice, "I don't have to tell you." But each demon eventually did.

I had not planned to take notes, but as the first demon began to reveal the information I asked for, it occurred to me that we might need to refer to this later. So grabbing a piece of paper and a pencil from the secretary's desk, I began a running record of what the demons said during the confrontations.

Most of the work the demons were doing in Paula's body and mind was manifested as symptoms or difficulties from which she was obviously suffering. The demons gave Paula headaches. .She had been suffering from headaches for several weeks before she went to the hospital. Demons prevented her from sleeping. They oppressed her with feelings of guilt and worthlessness. And they had tormented her with an almost irresistible urge to smoke in recent weeks.

We knew Paula had been having these symptoms before the encounters began. We were not shocked that various demons, when we demanded to know their assignments, assumed responsibility for causing them. There was a remarkable correlation between the symptoms as we knew them and the statements made by the demons.

Weeks before we even suspected the presence of demons or their influence in Paula's life, we had become aware of the physical weakness that had put her in the hospital several times during the first few months after we met her. She estimated that she had been in and out of hospitals some fifty times during her adult life, and her father verified this when I talked with him about it.

So much time spent in hospitals, with the resulting loss of employment, had left her and her two children with very little of this world's goods. She told me during one of her stays in the hospital that at times she envied other women her age who were better off, who had homes and furniture. About a year before I met her, she had placed her two children in foster homes because she felt they would have better care there than she could provide for them.

Since the double vision, slurred speech, and headaches had already plagued Paula during the three months prior to the first encounter in our trailer, these conditions became somewhat of a barometer. When two or more of these symptoms appeared, we knew a "storm" was probably imminent. The demons would take over before long. It was remarkable how suddenly these conditions could appear or disappear. One, two, or all three of these symptoms could come or go in a matter of minutes.

Here are the (fictitious) names of the eight demons and the work of each, as the information was revealed to us that Monday:

Dorothy: "I'm in charge here. I cause her not to sleep. I give her headaches. I give her nightmares. I cause her to smoke. I cause her to want to take drugs."

Ruby: "I cause her physical weakness. I give her feelings of guilt. I cause her to feel worthless. I cause her to faint. I make her have evil thoughts."

Barbara: "I make her irritable. I give her nightmares. I make her feel depressed."

Judy: "I make her smoke."

Jack: "I started it all. I make her have nightmares. I give her bad memories. I make her smoke."

Harold: "I bring back bad memories."

Raymond: "I take over her mind. I make her have evil thoughts."

"Unknown": "I give her double vision. I cause her sleeplessness. I make her speech slurred. I give her poor memory. I give her a bad temper. I make her feel worthless. I make her want to take pills."

43

Five

"I won't leave! No! No! I won't leave! I'll never leave her!" the demons screamed, repeating these objections over and over for fifteen or twenty minutes and at times accompanied by comments derogatory to God, the Bible, or the church.

Later, on the way back to her room, I told Paula her throat would probably be sore the next day.

"Why should my throat be sore?" she asked.

"Because you did quite a lot of yelling during the confrontation this afternoon."

Other than to tell me later that her throat was sore as I had predicted, she never referred to the matter again.

Several people came to the church to help prepare for the Vacation Bible School to begin a few days later. When some of them tried to enter the office where we were, Pastor Doyle slipped out and told them briefly what was happening. These people went immediately to one of the Sabbath School rooms and began a prayer season for Paula.

The confrontation sapped the physical and emotional vitality of all of us who participated, most of all Paula. She required rest between encounters. During these periods she frequently complained of having severe headaches and great thirst. So we kept damp

44

washcloths on her forehead and supplied her with plenty of water. During one encounter a demon caused Paula to cover her mouth and nostrils with the washcloth in an attempt to smother herself. There were several attempts to do the same thing with the pillow we kept under her head. At these times Paula seemed to have more than natural strength. At times it was all that several of us could do to wrest the articles from her grasp. We always had to be alert to any possible attempt to injure her or to take her life.

Some aspects of these encounters I still cannot explain. Several times, while the demons were in control, Paula would become suddenly aware of her physical needs. She would return to what seemed to be a normal state and would say, for example, "I have to use the bathroom." When she returned from the bathroom, the encounter would be resumed as though there had been no interruption. Later she could not recall these inter-ludes of normal behavior. At first I feared that she would lock herself in the bathroom. I imagined our having to break the door down to get her out, perhaps not even in time to prevent her from injuring herself before we could get to her. But of course, we had no choice but to let her use the restroom when she requested it.

On one of these occasions after she had been in the restroom for several minutes, we heard banging sounds coming from the room. I went to the door and called her name several times.

She did not respond. Instead, the banging continued. In view of the demons' repeated threat to kill her, I was concerned about what might be going on. I could imagine Paula banging her head against the wall or injuring herself in some other way. After calling and knocking several times with no answer, I opened the door. There stood Paula, banging on the window with a broom handle. Fortunately the screen was on the inside of the window so that the window could open outward, The broom handle had struck the screen instead of the window, and no damage had been done.

"What are you doing?" I asked.

"I thought maybe I could get out here."

"No, you can't," I said. Then I led her back to the office, and the encounter was resumed.

(We tried always to have at least one of our church ladies present at these confrontations, but this precaution was not possible on this occasion!)

Monday's confrontations were important because, as I have already indicated, on that day the demons identified themselves. We claimed God's promise of wisdom. (See James 1:5.) We asked that He not permit any of the demons to deceive us—so that we might know when all of them had identified themselves. When there was no more response from the reading of Matthew 10:1, 5-8, we assumed by faith that all of the demons present had been forced to identify themselves. God was good and answered our prayers. *No new demons were disclosed after Monday's encounters.*

Back at the motel Monday evening Paula said she was hungry; so we took her to a nearby drive-in and bought her some food to take to her room. I offered to ask Mrs. Allen to stay with her that night, but Paula said she was not afraid and she would be all right. There were no more disturbances that night.

Although it was rather late when I got home Monday night, I tried to call our conference president. When I learned he was out of the area, I called the conference secretary and requested that Paula's need be made the subject of special prayer at the staff worship the next morning. Tuesday morning I called "The Quiet Hour,"

46

"The Voice of Prophecy," and "Faith for Today," making the same request. In each case sympathetic persons told me that Paula would be remembered Thursday morning when these groups had their prayer sessions.

On Tuesday Paula again called for help. I took her to the church, where we met Pastor Paddock. While talking together, we experienced another encounter. But nothing seemed to be gained from that experience. Something seemed to be keeping Paula from gaining the victory. We felt that she must be holding something back from God even yet. There must still be some sin in her life that she had not confessed and forsaken. What else could keep God from giving her the victory?

Determined that I would do everything I could to cooperate with God in making that victory possible and remembering Christ's words, "Howbeit this kind goeth not out but by prayer and fasting" (Matthew 17:21), I decided that I would fast. And so I ate nothing Wednesday or Thursday.

Paula called for help about 2:30 Wednesday afternoon. The middle of the afternoon and about 1:30 in the morning were the times she needed help most often. I have wondered what significance, if any, may be attached to this. Could it be that these were the times in Paula's daily cycle when her metabolic rate was at its lowest ebb and that Satan took advantage of this? I don't know. But it must be more than a coincidence that these were often the times when she needed help.

Before I went to Paula's room, I called Pastor Paddock and asked him to meet me at the church, which he did. After I left, my wife called Brother Stiles; and he also met us. The three of us spent the rest of the afternoon in confrontations. But the experience was nearly a repetiton of Tuesday's, with no tangible evidence of

47

victory. We concluded the encounter just as people began to arrive at the church for prayer meeting. Pastor Paddock took Paula to her motel, with Brother Stiles following in his car.

I had charge of prayer meeting that night. Without going into a lot of details about Paula's need, we made her case the subject of special prayer.

After prayer meeting I went to Paula's motel. The other two men were still there, but Brother Stiles left soon after I arrived. When Pastor Paddock and I started to leave a few minutes later, Paula said, "Don't leave me alone tonight." Always before, she had refused my offer to arrange for someone to stay with her at night. I don't know why she didn't want to be left alone that particular night. I have never asked her.

"I can't stay with you here at night," I said.

"I know that."

"And Pastor Paddock can't stay here either."

"I know that too."

But both Pastor Paddock and I knew we could not leave Paula alone that night. I looked at him, and he looked at me. I am sure we were both thinking the same thing.

"You know we can't leave her," I said. "Why don't we both stay? If people don't understand and want to talk, they'll just have to talk."

I called my wife and explained the situation to her. Pastor Paddock was single and didn't have that responsibility. So I slept on the floor on one side of Paula's bed, and Pastor Paddock slept on the floor on the other side. We agreed to take turns sleeping and praying, but in actuality I think we both prayed more than we slept.

Paula hardly moved for several hours, and I thanked God that she was getting the sleep she badly needed. Then at 1:30 a.m. by my watch she roused.

Suddenly she sat up in bed. A voice which was not hers said, "I want to smoke."

"But this girl does not smoke," I replied.

"I know she doesn't. She knows it is wrong, but I am trying to make her think it is all right. I want to smoke. I am going to find a cigarette."

Paula got up, got her purse, and looked in it for a cigarette. But of course she found none. Then she went to the wastebasket and looked in it. Failing to find one there, she got back into bed.

"There's a vending machine across the way," the voice said. "Go get me a pack of cigarettes."

"No," I replied, "I won't get you any cigarettes."

"Look, I want to smoke. Just get me some cigarettes, and I will cooperate with you. I'll smoke just this much of the cigarette." Paula held up her hand with her finger and thumb a small fraction of an inch apart to indicate just how little she would smoke.

"No. The girl you are trying to control does not smoke, and I will not buy you any cigarettes."

"I'm thirsty. Get me a cold drink then. There's a machine that sells cold drinks too."

Thinking that perhaps Paula was thirsty, I said, "All right, I'll get you a cold drink."

"While you're there, get me some cigarettes too." The demon did not give up easily.

"No cigarettes," I replied.

But I did go across the way and get a cold drink, which Paula later drank. Given another opportunity, I believe I would deny the request for the cold drink just as I did the request for the cigarettes.

"Do you know what this demon said while you were gone?" Pastor Paddock asked when I came into the room with the drink.

"No, of course not. What did he say?"

49

"He said, 'This girl really loves the Lord. We are losing the battle.' "

"Praise the Lord!" I said. "I'm sure He is going to give Paula victory today."

Why did the demon voluntarily admit that he was losing the battle? I don't know. Neither do I know why the demons said and did other things that seemed contrary to their best interest. I don't know why the demons allowed Paula to let me into her room time after time and then rebuked themselves for doing it. I can account for some of these things only by assuming that God, who is more powerful than all the demons, limited their power and sometimes caused them to say things they may not have chosen to say.

I do know that the demon's statement that he and his fellows were losing the battle gave us great courage. Paula must have made a genuine commitment to the Lord that night, which opened the way for God to give her complete victory.

Paula drank the cold drink, settled down, and went back to sleep. There were no more disturbances that night, and Pastor Paddock and I left about six o'clock Thursday morning without waking Paula.

Six

Thursday morning about nine o'clock my wife and I took Paula a breakfast. She was sitting on her bed and seemed in good spirits. Wanting to encourage her, I told her that the demon had said he knew she really loved the Lord and that they, the demons, were losing the battle. "See, Paula," I said, "God is going to give you victory over these demons, and I believe He is going to do it today."

Somehow I felt that God would answer the prayers of all the people who were praying for Paula. This day had been set aside as a special day of prayer at "The Quiet Hour," "The Voice of Prophecy," "Faith for Today," and the conference office. Some of our church members also knew of Paula's need and were joining in this special day of prayer. Surely God would honor the prayers of His people. Of this I was confident.

"But what about the pills?" Paula asked. For several months Paula had been taking several different kinds of prescribed pills, but she wanted to be free from them.

The words she had spoken were hardly out of her mouth when she fell back on the bed. Her body writhed in a peculiar pattern. It was the most violent physical encounter Paula had so far experienced.

"In the name of the Lord Jesus Christ and as a minister of His gospel, I demand that you tell me who you are and what your work is."

"I am the Unknown Demon. I make her take pills. I hate you. Everything was going fine until you came along. Then I could control her. Now you have brought the battle out into the open. You are always here. Every time I open my eyes you are here. Why don't you go away?"

This tirade, with the exception of the reference to the use of pills, I had heard several times before, usually en route to the church with Paula.

Using Paula's telephone, my wife called our home and asked our daughter to call Pastor and Mrs. Doyle and Pastor Paddock. A few minutes later they all came to the motel.

By the time they arrived, Paula's confrontation with evil had become so violent that my wife and I had to hold her arms and shoulders to keep her on the bed and to prevent her from injuring herself. Screaming in the demon voice, she raised her hips and legs as high as she could off the bed and kicked with all her strength. She repeated this action over and over until she was exhausted, sometimes for ten or fifteen minutes. Then there would be a rest period of a minute or two before renewing the action. "No, no, I'll never leave her!" screamed the demon. "I've been in this girl a long time, and I'm not going to leave her now!"

In response we were constantly praying.

Paula's physical movements had become different from the previous ones. "This is what we have been waiting for," I told my wife. The movements showed a pattern or rhythm. The movements and loud vocal objections would reach a peak and then end. This would be repeated and repeated becoming louder and more violent as the encounter neared its end. This appeared to be a final protest just before the demon was forced out. Right up to the very end, each of the demons kept yelling, "I won't leave!" None left until this final climactic struggle took place. But then Paula's body suddenly relaxed. The demon's movements and vocal protests had built up to a climax and then suddenly stopped. We assumed that he had been forced to leave.

Fearing that the demons might try to deceive us into believing that they had fled when they hadn't, we prayed each time that God would not permit this to happen. Claiming the promise of James 1:5, we asked Him to give us the wisdom to know when victory had been gained over each demon so that we would not be deceived.

While Paula was "asleep," we would read again Matthew 10:1, 5-8. If the reading of this scripture produced no response, we assumed that the demon with whom we had been dealing had been forced to leave.

On two or three occasions reading these verses resulted in the same response that was produced by the reading when the confrontation was first induced. When this happened, we interpreted it to mean that the demon was still present. Then we repeated the entire procedure. In the cases of two demons it was necessary to repeat the process three times before the demons actually left. We are very thankful to God for His goodness in not permitting us to be deceived.

The experience of the first encounter on Thursday morning was so exhausting physically and emotionally to my wife that Pastor Paddock took her home after about an hour. The rest of us stayed until six o'clock that evening, when the series of confrontations ended.

After Paula had "slept" for a while following the first encounter Thursday morning, I asked God to wake her up.

53

"Dear Father," I prayed, "let your Holy Spirit speak to Paula's mind. If it is Your will, enable her to hear my voice just now."

"Paula," I said softly, "nod your head if you can hear me."

She nodded her head very slightly.

"Now, Paula, say 'Jesus.' "

"Jesus." The word was barely audible.

"Say 'help.' "

"Help." Her voice was more audible but still only a whisper.

"Say 'me.' "

"Me." Her voice was almost normal.

"Now say it all together as a prayer. 'Jesus, help me.' "

"Jesus—help—me." Her voice was becoming stronger.

She opened her eyes.

This procedure was followed after each of the confrontations, and God answered our prayer each time. The first time this happened, she was a bit puzzled about what had taken place and she was somewhat apprehensive about the whole thing; but after that she woke up each time with a smile.

"I am sure God is going to give you complete victory today," I told Paula when she was fully awake. "That is what you want, isn't it? We are prepared to stay here as long as necessary to give God opportunity to give you complete victory over every one of these demons. God wants to give you that victory, and we are here to cooperate with Him to make that possible. The only thing that can keep God from giving you the victory is a lack of faith and a lack of commitment on your part. Do you believe God *can* give you victory?"

"Yes."

"Do you believe He *will* give you victory?"

"Yes."

We then discussed again the necessity of her making the full commitment that would make victory possible.

"Now, Paula," I said at the end of the discussion, "we are going to ask God to do battle through the Holy Spirit and His angels with each of the demons still attempting to control you. We are going to ask Him to give you final victory over each of these demons. We believe He will give you that victory. But we will do this only if you agree. We will not do it against your will. Is this what you want?"

"Yes, that is what I want more than anything else in the world. I love God and His Son, Jesus so much. I know They will give me victory."

And so with Paula's consent we proceeded to induce another encounter. We followed much the same pattern that we had used in previous encounters, but our purpose now was to ask God to banish these demons from Paula's life.

We prayed that God would cause all those demon: who were not actively engaged in harassing or control- ling Paula to leave the building. We prayed that those demons who remained in the room might not be allowed to do harm to Paula in any way. Then we prayed that God would send the Holy Spirit and His angels to do battle with the enemy of Paula's soul. We acknowl- edged that this was a battle none of us could fight; we were entirely dependent upon God for victory. We prayed that He would give Paula not a partial victory, but a complete victory over every one of the demons. And we prayed again that God would fulfill His promise and give us knowledge that would enable us to know when the demons had been cast out, so that we would not be deceived.

When we finished praying, I read again from Matthew 10:1, 5-8. "And when he had called unto him his twelve disciples, *he gave them power against unclean spirits, to cast them out,* and to heal all manner of sickness, and all manner of disease.... These twelve Jesus sent forth, and commanded them saying, Go not unto the way of the Gentiles, and into any city of the Samaritans enter ye not: But go rather to the lost sheep of the house of Israel. And as ye go, preach, saying, The kingdom of heaven is at hand. Heal the sick, cleanse the lepers, raise the dead, *cast out devils:* freely ye have received, freely give."

In each case, when the expression "cast out devils" was read, the confrontation would begin. Paula's eyes would close. Her arms and legs would begin to move, only slightly at first; but this movement would increase within a few seconds until the action would become quite violent. These movements were always accompanied by vocal objections, "No, no, I won't leave! I don't have to leave!" Both the bodily movements and the vocalization would increase in intensity until they reached a climax. Then suddenly the voice would cease and Paula's body would relax in what appeared to be a peaceful sleep.

We followed the same procedure with each of the eight demons, always with the same result.

As soon as the encounter was under way and we knew that a demon was manifesting himself, I would take steps to gain the information we needed.

"In the name of Jesus Christ whose blood was shed for Paula's sins, I demand that you tell me your name."

And in every instance the name would be given, although sometimes this information was revealed only after there had been some objection. In every case the name was the same as one of the names that had been given to us during the encounter the previous Monday.

Once we had learned the demon's name, I would demand in the name of Jesus that he be quiet and stop talking. Always he obeyed. What wonderful power there is in the name of our Jesus! The demon would continue to object to having to leave, but he would make no further attempts to carry on a conversation with us.

Then I would demand, always in the name of Jesus, that the demon be forced to tell us what assignment he was carrying out in Paula's mind or body. This information was always revealed, and it always corresponded to the information that had been given during Monday's encounter.

When these two pieces of information had been gained—the demon's name and his work—I would next demand in Jesus' name that he be forced to leave.

"In the name of the Lord Jesus Christ who has shed His blood to cover Paula's sins and who has already won the victory over Satan at the cross, I command that demon So-and-So leave Paula's mind and body."

None of the demons left immediately. "Satan and his angels are unwilling to lose their prey. They contend and battle with holy angels, and the conflict is severe." 1T 301. "Satan will not yield one inch of ground except as he is driven back by the power of heavenly messengers." GC 559.

After having witnessed the evidence of this battle, I can verify the fact that the battle is very real and very severe. It is not a pleasant sight to see. But eventually the demon would be forced to leave, and Paula would relax.

After a few minutes rest following each encounter I would ask God to wake Paula up again. Then we would give her some more time to relax before we started the next confrontation. During these interludes Paula carried on a normal conversation. Several times she said, "Pray that God will free me from the pills." She had a great desire to be free from the drugs prescribed for her, and she was very happy when God answered our prayers and gave her that victory.

After the period of rest we repeated the entire procedure, and another demon would identify himself and his work and eventually be cast out.

The first demon who identified himself that Thursday morning made a curious and interesting statement: "When we leave, it will be in ascending order of importance," he said.

His statement disclosed several interesting facts worthy of our notice. In the first place he was acknowledging that the demons were going to have to leave. They knew they were already defeated. It was only a matter of time, but they were determined to stay until forced out. Thank God for a Saviour who has already won the battle! The demon's statement also indicated that the least important or least powerful of the demons would leave first, and the most powerful would leave last. This order is of course quite logical and natural. A friend of mine told me of a case where the demons actually argued among themselves as to which one should be the next to leave.

Of course, we have no real way of proving which demon was the most powerful or the least powerful; and we were not particularly concerned with the order of their leaving, so long as they all left. At least there was no arguing over the order of their exit in Paula's case.

According to my notes on Thursday's encounters the demons identified themselves and left in the following order: Harold, Ruby, Judy, Barbara, and Jack were the first five to leave. Raymond was the next to leave, but he left only after three different confrontations. Dorothy left next. The Unknown Demon was the last, and he required two separate encounters.

By Thursday evening we had experienced encounters with all of the eight demons who had identified themselves and their assignments the previous Monday. We were getting no more responses from the reading of Matthew 10, and we felt that God had given Paula the victory. She looked better than she had for several weeks. Her eyes were bright, and her speech was no longer slurred. She still had a headache, but we thought it was probably the natural result of what she had experienced that day. It had been a grueling experience, and all of us were emotionally and physically exhausted. I offered to arrange for someone to stay with Paula that night, but again she declined. So about 6:30 p.m., after another short period of prayer, we all left to go to our homes and some rest.

Seven

Looking back on Thursday's experience, I believe we should have taken a cue from the fact that Paula still had a headache at the end of the day and realized that there may still have been a demon present.

Paula called me Thursday night. "Come and help me! The devil is back, and he is making me break things, and I can't help it!"

"I'll be right there!"

I woke my wife and asked her to call Pastor Paddock and Brother Stiles, and to have them meet me at the church as soon as possible. Because of the urgency I did not take time to dress, but I put on a robe over my pajamas and left. When I knocked on Paula's door a little later, she let me in as usual. Neither she nor her room was a pleasant sight. The large mirror that had been fastened to the wall with an adhesive material had been completely pulled off, leaving several large cavities where plaster board had come off with it. The mirror itself lay smashed and scattered over the floor. Also on the floor were all the things that had previously been on the shelf under the mirror: a radio and a clock which we had loaned to Paula; several dishes from which she had eaten; hair curlers, and numerous other small personal items. And in the center of all this debris stood Paula—her face drawn and her eyes glazed, as they always were when the demons were in control.

I do not remember what she said when I first entered the room. But when I asked her to get into the car so we could go to the church, she did not object but cooperated as usual. During the trip to the church the demon volunteered some information.

"My name is Raymond. I hate you. You are interfering again with my work. Why did I let you in that room? That was a mistake."

All of this I had heard before. I prayed that God would cause him to be quiet, and there was no more talking.

Paula and I had not been at the church very long before Brother Stiles and Pastor Paddock arrived. As we had done before, we prayed that the Holy Spirit and the good angels would do battle with the evil angels. These demons who were the last to leave, the most powerful ones, put up a terrific fight, a more prolonged and more physically and verbally violent than any before. It seemed as though they would never give up.

When Thursday night's session was finally concluded, we three men agreed on one thing: Paula must not go back to that motel room again. It was associated with too many bad experiences, and it was just not a good place for her to be, under the circumstances. But what was the alternative?

We eventually agreed that she should go back to our trailer. She would have some privacy there, and yet she would not be entirely alone. She would be near us in case she needed help. This the three of us decided while Paula was still asleep; so she did not know of our decision. It was agreed that I would take her home to our trailer while Pastor Paddock and Brother Stiles went back to Paula's room and cleaned up the debris.

So Paula and I headed south on Holiday Avenue. I still had not told her about our plans. When we got to Randolph Road, I turned left toward our home rather than right toward Paula's motel. Although she did not remember this night's events the next morning, she realized at the time that I had turned the opposite way from her room.

"Where are we going?" she asked.

"We feel that it is best for you not to stay in that motel room any longer. I am going to take you back to our trailer."

"I don't want to go back to the trailer. I won't stay there. If you make me go there, I'll run off. Then you won't know where I am."

Just then the warning light on the dash told me the car was low on gasoline. My car was relatively new, and I had never run out of gas; so I had no idea how far I could go after the light came on. But I had no desire to run out of gas then, of all times.

It was about one o'clock Friday morning. I was dressed in pajamas and a robe. Before I had taken Paula to the church, I had looked in her room for a robe for her to put on; but I had not found one; so she was dressed only in pajamas. These circumstances combined with Paula's "problem" would have made it very awkward to be stranded beside the road, to say the least.

I turned north toward the boulevard, hoping to see the lights of an open station. But when I reached the boulevard, I could still see no lights; so I headed for the next town, about five miles away. After driving about two miles I still did not see any open station. But I did see a highway patrol car parked beside the road. I pulled in ahead of the car and walked back. After apologizing for my unusual attire I started to explain my need. But before I could say very much, the officer smiled.

"Yes," he said, "I know who you are."

Then I remembered meeting him several weeks earlier under perfectly legitimate, but less awkward, circumstances.

"The closest open station is on Holiday Avenue, just north of the boulevard."

Of course! I should have known. I remembered it as soon as he mentioned it. In fact I had passed the open station on the way from the church not too long before.

"I'll follow you, in case you have any problem," the officer said.

He did follow me, and I appreciated his presence. Fortunately we did not need his help, and he honked his horn as I pulled into the open station.

After filling the tank I drove Paula back to her room. Pastor Paddock and Brother Stiles were just finishing the job of cleaning up the debris. Since Paula had refused to move back into our trailer, we discussed again what we should do about her housing, and we finally called another motel and arranged for Paula to stay there. So we loaded Paula's few belongings into Pastor Paddock's car, and in a few minutes we had her settled in her new room. Then we went to our homes for some rest during what remained of the night.

The next morning I thought it might be well to see how Paula was doing. I knocked on her door.

"Am I glad to see you!" she greeted.

She told me that she had been frightened when she woke up that morning in what was to her a strange room. Although she had seemed quite normal after the encounter the night before, she remembered nothing of what had happened from the time she called me for help until she woke up in her new room. I explained to her that there had been another encounter the night before, that we had gone to the church, and that we thought it best for her not to return to her former room.

Paula never mentioned it to me, but my wife told me later that Paula had called just after I left the house that morning.

"I'm scared," Paula said. "I'm in a different room, and I don't know where I am. Am I still in the same place?"

"Yes, Paula, you are in the same town. You're in a different motel, but everything will be all right," my wife assured her. "You don't need to be frightened."

I must have knocked on Paula's door soon after she finished talking with my wife on the phone.

After leaving Paula I went to her former motel. I told the manager that Paula had experienced another "problem" in her room the night before and that the mirror had been broken. I told him that since I was not there at the time the damage had been done, I did not know exactly how it had happened. Paula is a small woman; and I still don't know how she managed to pull that large mirror off the wall, taking large globs of the plasterboard with it. The most plausible explanation of course is that the demon supplied the strength.

While the manager and I talked, we walked to the room. The debris, of course, was gone; and except for the absence of the mirror and presence of the craters on the wall where the mirror had been, the room looked fine.

"The occupant will have to pay for the installation of a new mirror," the manager said. This fact I had taken for granted.

Of course I told him that Paula no longer occupied the room but that she would contact him regarding the costs.

Eight

Friday night passed without any interruption and gave me the first full night's sleep in more than a week. I was so sure that God had given Paula a complete victory that at my suggestion our Sabbath congregation sang "Praise God, From Whom All Blessings Flow." After church Mrs. Allen and I enjoyed a delicious dinner at the Stiles home.

After leaving the Stileses in the middle of the afternoon, we went to Paula's room. Dr. and Mrs. Smith were already there, and we all had a pleasant visit. We read some promises from the Bible and had a short season of prayer, and then the four of us left.

About an hour later Paula called. "Pastor Allen, the devil is after me again. Why doesn't he leave me alone? Please come."

"Phone the Stileses and ask them to meet us at the church right away," I called to my wife as I hurried to the car.

They responded to her call, as usual.

Paula opened the door when I knocked. But what I saw frightened me. Both wrists were bloody, and in her hand she held the pull-off seal of a soft-drink can, which she had used to cut herself.

"Paula, give me what you have in your hand." She

65

gave it to me without any protest. "Now, show me your wrists." She extended her arms. I took her hands and looked more carefully at her wrists. The cuts were superficial, looking at the first glance worse than they actually were.

"You'd better get in the car with me."

"Where are we going?"

"We are going to the church again."

"Why are we going to the church now? I'm tired of going to the church."

"Because we need to talk and pray."

"Are you sure you're not going to take me to the hospital?"

"No, I won't take you to the hospital. I promise that we will go to the church."

Thus assured, she got into the car. On the way to the church the demon in control began to talk as he frequently did during these trips. Usually he said very much the same thing each time. This time was no exception.

"I am the Unknown Demon, and I hate you."

"Why do you hate me?"

"Because you have interfered with my work. I have been controlling this girl for years. Everything was going fine until you came along. Now the battle is out in the open. But I will never leave her. Never! I will make her lose her job, and eventually I will kill her."

At this point I decided he had said enough, and I asked in the name of Jesus that he not be allowed to say any more.

My prayer was answered, and he said no more until the encounter began at the church. As I drove, I prayed constantly for our safety. I was aware of the many threats that had been made to kill Paula, and I certainly did not want the demon to cause her to grab the steering wheel or do some other hazardous thing in an attempt to carry out the threat while I was driving.

Usually when I arrived with Paula at the church, I took her with me to the church door and then unlocked it and led her up the steps to the office. This time I left Paula sitting in the car while I went to unlock the church door. Some weeks earlier, before the confrontations, she had left a nearly full bottle of her prescription pills in our car. I had paid no attention to them, and they were still there. As I started back to the car after opening the church door, I saw Paula with one hand to her mouth and the other hand holding the bottle. I knew instantly what she was doing. She had opened the bottle and poured all the capsules into her hand and was in the act of putting them into her mouth when I opened the car door and knocked her hand away from her mouth.

"Spit them out, Paula! Spit them out!" I shouted.

She went through the motions of spitting, but nothing came out. I thanked God in my heart that I had been able to get to the car in time.

We went into the church, and I washed the blood from Paula's wrists. There were big red scratches on both arms, but no real injury had been done.

I had just finished taking care of Paula's wrists when Kenneth and Dorothy Stiles arrived, and we soon brought on the confrontation. This encounter was the most severe and prolonged of them all, as though the demon was fighting for his life. In one sense he was; he was fighting for his life in Paula. It seemed as if the encounter would never end, but eventually there was a crescendo of action and repeated cries of "I won't leave!" and then Paula relaxed. Repeated reading of Matthew 10:1, 5-8 brought no response, and we thanked God for the victory.

While Paula was still sleeping, I went out and swept

up the capsules that had been scattered on the floor of the car and on the blacktop when I knocked them from her hand.

A little later we asked God to wake Paula up, and I took her to her room. Shortly after we left the church, she noticed the scratches on her wrists.

"Did I do that?" she asked. But her tone indicated that she already knew the answer.

Nine

The next day, Sunday afternoon, Paula called. "Pastor Allen, I think maybe you should take me some place where I can be watched. I feel as though I am going to pieces. I don't think I should be left alone."

This was a new turn. Always before, with the exception of the night Pastor Paddock and I had stayed with her, Paula had insisted on being left alone. I was glad to hear her say what she did, feeling that she may have been entering a new phase of her experience, in which she was at least aware of her feelings. In fact, I had anticipated this situation; and I had already discussed with Dorothy Stiles the possibility of Paula's staying with her and Kenneth for a while.

"I'll come right over, and we'll talk about it," I told Paula.

I then called Dorothy, and we finalized plans for me to take Paula out to the Stiles home. They live in a quiet semirural area, and I felt that they and the environment could do Paula a lot of good.

But when I saw Paula a few minutes later, she had a different idea.

"I need a tranquilizer," she said. "Take me to a doctor who will give me a tranquilizer, or I'm afraid I'll go to pieces and end up in a mental hospital."

I felt she was entering a critical time. If with God's help she could survive the next few days on her own without medication, she would have won the battle. But if she resorted to tranquilizers now, much that had been gained would be lost.

"Paula, we have prayed that God would deliver you from pills, and we must have faith to believe that He has done that. God does not want you to resort to tranquilizers now. I want you to come with me. I am going to take you out to the Stiles's home. It's out in the country, where it's quiet; and I know you will learn to love Dorothy and Kenneth. They are lovely people. Will you come with me and give it a try for a few days?"

"I'll go anywhere you think I should go, but I need a tranquilizer."

So we drove out to the Stiles home in the country. The only time Paula had met the Stileses was when she was having an encounter. Since she did not remember these experiences, they were strangers to her. I thought it was best for me to stay and visit for a while until Paula was somewhat at ease, and then I prepared to leave.

"Don't forget to find a doctor who will give me a tranquilizer." This was the last thing Paula said to me as I started toward my car.

"I'll call a doctor just as soon as I get home," I promised; "and then I'll come back to see you."

I kept my promise. As soon as I got home, I called Dr. Smith and explained the situation to him.

"She should have no tranquilizers," he advised.

Other matters demanded my attention, and I returned to the Stiles home later than I had intended. It was early evening. Paula said I had deserted her and expressed her unhappiness with me for not returning sooner.

I assured her that I had not intended to be gone so long and that in a day or so she would enjoy it there.

When she asked about the tranquilizers, I told her that since it was Sunday we had better wait until the next day, when it would be easier to find a doctor. I hoped and prayed that before the next day passed she would no longer feel the need for medication.

Perhaps Dorothy sensed Paula's timidity. Anyway, for some reason she suggested to me privately that it might be a good idea for me to spend the night there.

"That's all right with me if you will call my wife and explain the situation to her," I said.

She did this, and then I talked to my wife also. So that night while Paula slept in the guest room, I slept on the davenport in the family room, just down the hall. The night passed uneventfully.

We woke up to a bright, beautiful, clear day. The Stileses were already up and about when I got up, but Paula was still asleep.

"Dorothy, don't let Paula sleep any longer," I suggested. "Go in and wake her up now while it is so beautiful outside, and take her out to the garden."

"That's a good idea," Dorothy agreed. "I'll take her out to the garden, and we'll pick some strawberries."

Dorothy went to Paula's room (Paula told me later) and kissed her on the cheek to awaken her and then knelt by her bed and prayed a short prayer.

"That was one of the most beautiful experiences I have ever had," Paula told me.

Paula put on a robe, and she and Dorothy went out into the garden. No strawberries were ready to pick, but they did bring in some ripe, red, luscious tomatoes. I am sure that just getting out into the garden in the early morning sun had great therapeutic value for Paula. Never again to this day has she mentioned to me the need of tranquilizers. When the ladies came in from the garden, we had worship; and then Dorothy and Paula

71

prepared a delicious breakfast, which we all enjoyed.

That day was the beginning of a new life for Paula. Before the day ended, a bond of love had begun to draw her and the Stileses together. She made her home with them for several weeks until she found a rental that met her needs. I am as certain that God led Paula to Dorothy and Kenneth Stiles as I am that He delivered her from the power of Satan.

As I write these words, another spring has come and gone and more than a year has passed since we experienced that first encounter in the trailer. The events of that summer seem unreal and far away. Today Paula is a new person in Christ Jesus, completely free from the evil forces which once controlled her. She no longer suffers from headaches, weakness, or sleeplessness. She has no depression, resentment, or feelings of guilt. There is no desire to smoke or to take pills. All these things came to an end when the demons were cast out.

Paula is employed at a large hospital, where she enjoys her work. Her happiness increased when in the spring she flew east to bring back her children, from whom she had been separated for two years.

Two portions of Scripture are especially meaningful to Paula. The first is the series of promises we often shared during the times she was in the hospital. It helped to bolster her faith when her courage was low and the outlook was dark.

"Trust in the Lord, and do good; so shalt thou dwell in the land, and verily thou shalt be fed. Delight thyself also in the Lord; and he shall give thee the desires of thine heart. Commit thy way unto the Lord; trust also in him; and he shall bring it to pass." Psalm 37:3-5.

The second is equally inspirational. "When he was come into the ship, he that had been possessed with the devil prayed him that he might be with him. Howbeit

Jesus suffered him not, but saith unto him, Go home to thy friends, and *tell them how great things the Lord hath done for thee, and hath had compassion on thee."* Mark 5:18, 19.

Paula feels a special kinship to the man of Gadara. Both were delivered from demon possession.

Praise God!

Appendix A

Quotations From Ellen G. White
on Demon Possession

The following quotations on the subject of demon possession have been gleaned from Ellen White's writings. In no way do they represent a thorough study of the material available from this source. In fact, they merely scratch the surface. However, in reviewing Paula Green's experience in light of what I have found on the subject from the pen of inspiration, I have discovered no area where Paula's experience and the instructions from the spirit of prophecy are not compatible.

In the interest of brevity, I have quoted only the sentence or sentences that make the point to be emphasized. I would suggest that the serious reader study each of these quotations in its context. I would also encourage the reading of chapters 31 and 32 of *The Great Controversy*. Italics are supplied.

Demons actually inhabit human bodies and control their organs:

"The fact that men have been possessed with demons, is clearly stated in the New Testament. *The persons thus afflicted were not merely suffering with disease from natural causes.* Christ had perfect understanding of that with which He was dealing, and *He* recognized the direct presence and agency of evil spirits."—*The Great Controversy*, p. 514.

"*The bodies of human beings, made for the dwelling place of God, had* [in Christ's time] *become the habitation of demons. The senses, the nerves, the passions, the organs of men, were worked by supernatural agencies in the indulgence of the vilest lust."—The Desire of Ages*, p. 36.

Satan hates every human being:

"We have a powerful enemy, and *not only does he hate every human being* made in the image of God, but *with bitterest enmity he hates God and His only begotten Son Jesus Christ."—Fundamentals of Christian Education*, p. 299.

Demons are struggling for control in every one of us:

"He [Jesus] knows that *a demon power is struggling in every soul,* striving for the mastery, but Jesus came to break the power of Satan and to set the captives free."—*My Life Today*, p. 300.

"We should ever keep in mind that *unseen agencies are at work, both evil and good, to take control of the mind.* They act with unseen yet effectual power. . . . The great adversary of souls, the devil, and his angels are continually laboring to accomplish our destruction."—*The Adventist Home*, p. 405.

"Satan is busy every moment, going to and fro, walking up and down in the earth, *seeking whom he may devour.*" 5T 294.

Satan is gathering thousands under his control:

"*Satan takes possession of the minds of men today.* In my labors in the cause of God, *I have again and again met those who have been possessed, and in the name of the Lord I have rebuked the evil spirit."—Selected Messages,* bk. 2, p. 353.

"The condition of things in the world shows that

troublous times are right upon us. . . . *Men possessed of demons are taking the lives of men, women, and little children.* Men have become infatuated with vice, and every species of evil prevails." 9T 11

"He [Satan] flatters men with the pleasing fable that there is no rebellious foe, no deadly enemy that they need to guard against, and that the existence of a personal devil is all fiction; and while he thus hides his existence, *he is gathering thousands under his control."—Confrontation,* pp. 35, 36.

The battle with Satan is very real:

"*Satan is Christ's personal enemy.* . . . If our eyes could be opened to discern the fallen angels at work with those who feel at ease and consider themselves safe, we would not feel so secure. *Evil angels are upon our track every moment.*" 1T 302

"*It is not a mimic battle in which we are engaged. We are waging a warfare upon which hang eternal results. We have unseen enemies to meet. Evil angels are striving for the dominion of every being."—The Ministry of Healing,* p. 128.

"Satan and his angels are unwilling to lose their prey. *They contend and battle with holy angels, and the conflict is severe."—Messages to Young People,* p. 60.

Every one of us is controlled either by God or by Satan:

"*We must be daily controlled by the Spirit of God or we are controlled by Satan.*" 5T 102

"*Every man, woman and child that is not under control of the Spirit of God is under the influence of Satan's sorcery.*" MYP 278

Satan will work with his greatest success as we near the end of time:

"None are in greater danger from the influence of evil spirits than those who, notwithstanding the direct and simple testimony of the Scriptures, deny the existence and agency of the devil and his angels. . . . This is why, *as we approach the close of time, when Satan is to work with greatest power to deceive and destroy,* he spreads everywhere the belief that he does not exist. It is his policy to conceal himself and his manner of working." GC 516

"As we near the close of time, the human mind is more readily affected by Satan's devices." 1T 293.

We should become as well informed as possible regarding Satan's devices:

"If God has granted to His children promise of grace and protection, it is because there are mighty agencies of evil to be met—*agencies numerous, determined, and untiring, of whose malignity and power none can safely be ignorant or unheeding."* GC 513

"So long as we are ignorant of their [the devil and his angels'] wiles, they have almost inconceivable advantage." GC 516

"Satan is well aware that the weakest soul who abides in Christ is more than a match for the hosts of darkness, and that, *should he reveal himself openly, he would be met and resisted."* GC 530

"There are evil angels at work all around us, but *because we do not discern their presence with our natural vision we do not consider as we should the reality of their existence as set forth in the word of God."* 5T 533

"There is nothing that the great deceiver fears so much as that we shall become acquainted with his devices." GC 516

Satan is a master workman with much experience:

"He [Satan] has been growing more artful, and *has learned the most successful manner in which to come to the children of men with his temptations."* 1T 342

"Satan is a master workman. His infernal wisdom he

77

employs with good success. . . . *Our adversary, the devil, is not void of wisdom or strength.''* 2T 172

Satan studies our individual weaknesses:

"Satan studies every indication of the frailty of human nature, *he marks the sins which each individual is inclined to commit,* and then he takes care that opportunities shall not be wanting to gratify the tendency of evil.'' GC 555

Satan does not always come as a roaring lion:

"The enemy does not always come as a roaring lion; he frequently appears as an angel of light, assuming friendly airs, presenting peculiar temptations which it is difficult for the inexperienced to withstand.'' 4T 207

"He [Satan[*does not always wear the ferocious look of the lion,* but when he can work to better effect, he transforms himself into an angel of light. *He can readily exchange the roar of the lion for the most persuasive arguments or for the softest whisper.''* 2T 287

"Good people" can be harrassed by demons:

"There were hours when the whisperings of demons tortured his [John the Baptist's] *spirit, and the shadow of a terrible fear crept over him.''* DA 216

"Satan summons all his forces and throws his whole power into the combat. Why is it that he meets with no greater resistance? Why are the soldiers of Christ so sleepy and indifferent? Because they have so little real connection with Christ; because they are so destitute of His Spirit. Sin is not to them repulsive and abhorrent, as it was to their Master. They do not meet it, as did Christ, with decisive and determined resistance. They do not realize the exceeding evil and malignity of sin, and they are blinded both to the character and the power of the prince of darkness. There is little enmity against Satan and his works, because there is so great ignorance concerning his power and malice, and the vast extent of his warfare against Christ and His church. . . . Among professed Christians, and even among ministers of the gospel, there is heard scarcely a reference to Satan, except perhaps an incidental mention in the pulpit. They overlook the evidences of his continual activity and success; they neglect the many warnings of his subtlety; they seem to ignore his very existence.

". . . He is intruding his presence in every department of the household, in every street of our cities, in the churches, in the national councils, in the courts of justice, perplexing, deceiving, seducing, everywhere ruining the souls and bodies of men, women, and children, breaking up families, sowing hatred, emulation, strife, sedition, murder. And the Christian world seem to regard these things as though God had appointed them and they must exist." GC 507, 508

"When Christ revealed to Peter the time of trial and suffering that was just before Him, and Peter replied, Be it far from thee, Lord: this shall not be unto thee' (Matt. 16:22), the Saviour commanded, 'Get thee behind me, Satan (Matt. 16:23). *Satan was speaking through Peter, making him act the part of the tempter. Satan's presence was unsuspected by Peter, but Christ could detect the presence of the deceiver, and His rebuke to Peter He addressed to the real foe.*" 2SM 353; see also DA 416

We have no defense against Satan in our own strength:

"The power and malice of Satan and his host might justly alarm us were it not that we may find shelter and deliverance in the superior power of our Redeemer. We carefully secure our houses with bolts and locks to protect our property and our lives from evil men; but we seldom think of the evil angels who are constantly seeking access to us, and *against whose attacks we have, in our own strength, no method of defense.* GC 517

"Man is Satan's captive and is naturally inclined to follow his suggestions and do his bidding. *He has in himself no power to oppose effectual resistance to evil.* It is only as Christ abides in him by living faith, influencing his desires and strengthening him with strength from above, that many may venture to face so terrible a foe. Every other means of defense is utterly vain. *It is only through Christ that Satan's power is limited.*" 5T 294

We can come under Satan's control in many ways:

"Satan has summoned the hosts of darkness to war against the saints. We can not afford to be indifferent to his attacks. *He comes in many ways,* and we must have clear spiritual discernment that we may be able to discern when he is seeking to gain possession of our minds."—*Our High Calling,* p. 19.

Satan may gain entrance through intemperance and frivolity:

"The cause of this [demon-possessed] man's affliction . . . was in his own life. [See Luke 4:31-37.] He had been fascinated with the pleasure of sin and thought to make life a grand carnival. *Intemperance and frivolity perverted the noble attributes of his nature, and Satan took entire control of him.*" MH 91

Satan may gain entrance through uncontrolled thoughts and feelings:

"*You should keep off from Satan's enchanted ground* and not allow your minds to be swayed from allegiance to God. . . . *When you decide that as Christians you are not required to restrain your thoughts and feelings you are brought under the influence of evil angels and invite their presence and their control.*" 5T 310

Satan may gain entrance when we tamper with him and walk on his ground:

"In this degenerate age, *Satan holds control over*

those who depart from the right and venture upon his ground. He exercises his power upon such in an alarming manner. . . . Some, I was shown, gratify their curiosity and *tamper with the devil.* They have no real faith in spiritualism and would start back with horror at the idea of being mediums. Yet they venture and *place themselves in a position where Satan can exercise his power upon them.* Such do not mean to enter deep into this work, but they know not what they are doing. *They are venturing on the devil's ground and tempting him to control them.* This powerful destroyer considers them his lawful prey and exercises his power upon them, and that against their will. When they wish to control themselves they cannot. *They yielded their minds to Satan, and he will not release his claims,* but holds them captive. No power can deliver the ensnared soul but the power of God in answer to the earnest prayers of His followers." 1T 299

Satan may gain entrance when we knowingly disregard God's commandments:

"There are multitudes today as truly under the power of evil spirits as was in the demoniac of Capernaum. *All who willfully depart from God's commandments are placing themselves under the control of Satan.* Many a man tampers with evil, thinking that he can break away at pleasure; but he is lured on and on, until he finds himself controlled by a will stronger than his own. He cannot escape its mysterious power. Secret sin or master passion may hold him a captive as helpless as was the demoniac of Capernaum." MH 92, 93

We may hold communion with evil spirits by manifesting un-Christlike traits:

"When men reveal the opposite traits [from the Christian], *when they are proud, vain, frivolous, worldly-minded, avaricious, unkind, censorious,* we

81

need not be told with whom they are associating, who is their most intimate friend. *They may not believe in witchcraft; but, notwithstanding this, they are holding communion with an evil spirit."* 5T 225

We may fall prey to Satan when we cherish known sins:

"All who indulge sinful traits of character, or willfully cherish a known sin, are inviting the temptations of Satan. They separate themselves from God and from the watchcare of His angels; *as the evil one presents his deceptions, they are without defense and fall an easy prey.* GC 558-559

Unpleasant words spoken in the home open the door for evil angels:

"Parents, let the words you speak to your children be kind and pleasant, that angels may have your help in drawing them to Christ. A thorough reformation is needed in the home church. Let it begin at once. Let all grumbling and fretting and scolding case. *Those who fret and scold shut out the angels of heaven and open the door to evil angels."* AH 441

Unconverted children are an easy prey for Satan:

"Children who have not experienced the cleansing power of Jesus are the lawful prey of the enemy, and the evil angels have easy access to them. . . . By faithful and untiring efforts of the parents, and the blessing and grace bestowed upon the children in response to the prayers of the parents, the power of the evil angels may be broken and a sanctifying influence shed upon the children. Thus the powers of darkness will be driven back."—*Counsels to Parents, Teachers, and Students,* p. 118.

Satan assigns a work to each of his angels:

"Satan assigns to each of his angels a part to act. He enjoins upon them all to be sly, artful, cunning."— *Early Writings,* p. 90.

Demon of unkindness:

"Some who profess to be servants of Christ have so long cherished *the demon of unkindness* that they seem to love the unhallowed element and to take pleasure in speaking words that displease and irritate."—*The Sanctified Life*, p. 16.

Demon of intemperance:

"*The demon of intemperance* is of giant strength, and is not easily conquered."—*Temperance*, p. 176.

"Indulgence in intoxicating liquor places a man wholly under the control of *the demon who devised this stimulant* in order to deface and destroy the moral image of God." Te 32

"He [Christ] can give us help to conquer even this *demon of intemperance*."—*Child Guidance*, p. 401.

Demon of jealousy:

"*The demon of jealousy* entered the heart of the king [Saul] when David received praise for victory in battle."—*Patriarchs and Prophets*, p. 650.

Demon of passion:

"The intelligence [knowledge of David's where-abouts] aroused *the demon of passion* that had been slumbering in Saul's breast." PP 668

Demon of selfishness:

"If he [Judas] would open his heart to Christ, divine grace would banish *the demon of selfishness*, and even Judas might become a subject of the kingom of God." DA 294

Demon of strife:

"If the law of God is obeyed, *the demon of strife* will be kept out of the family." AH 106

Demon of nicotine:

"Men professing godliness offer their bodies upon Satan's altar and *burn the incense of tobacco to his satanic majesty*. Does this statement seem severe? Certainly, the offering is presented to some deity. As God is pure and holy, and will accept nothing defiling in its character, He must refuse this expensive, filthy, and unholy sacrifice; therefore, *we conclude that Satan is the one who claims the honor.*" SL 31

Demon of affliction:

"*Satan will go to the extent of his power to harass, tempt, and mislead God's people. . . . In a marvelous manner will he affect the bodies* of those who are naturally inclined to do his bidding." 1T 341, 342

"*Satan's influence is constantly exerted upon men to distract the senses, control the mind for evil, and incite to violence and crime. He weakens the body,* darkens the intellect, and debases the soul." DA 341

"It is not safe for you to trust to your impressions and feelings. . . . *Your imagination and nerves have been under the control of demons.* . . . You may, and frequently do, let down the bars and invite the enemy in, and *he controls your thoughts and actions,* while you are really deceived and flatter yourself that you are in favor with God." 3T 418

Demons take delight in misery and destruction:

"*Their* [evil angels] *only delight is in misery and destruction.*" GC 517

"*The ruin of souls is his* [Satan's] *only delight, their destruction his only employment;* and shall we act as though we were paralyzed?" 5T 384

Satan does not hesitate to do all he can to win and retain his captives:

"*The spirits of darkness will battle for the soul once under their dominion.*" DA 259

"*He* [Satan] *will not hesitate to engage all his energies and call to his aid all his evil host to wrest a single human being from the hand of Christ. . . . Satan and his angels are unwilling to lose their prey. They contend*

and battle with holy angels, and the conflict is severe."
1T 301

"Satan will not yield one inch of ground except as he is driven back by the power of heavenly messengers." GC 559

Christ cast out demons by the power of His word:

"It was by His word that Jesus healed disease and cast out demons."—Gospel Workers, p. 250.

Christ addressed the demons as intelligent beings:

"The daughter of the Syrophoenician woman was grievously vexed with a devil, *whom Jesus cast out by His word.* Mark 7:26-30. 'One possessed with a devil, blind, and dumb' (Matthew 12:22); a youth who had a dumb spirit, that oftentimes 'cast him into the fire, and into the waters, to destroy him,' (Mark 9:17-27); the maniac who, tormented by 'a spirit of an unclean devil' (Luke 4:33-36), disturbed the Sabbath quiet of the synagogue at Capernaum—all were healed by the compassionate Saviour, *In nearly every instance, Christ addressed the demon as an intelligent entity,* commanding him to come out of his victim and to torment him no more." GC 515, 516

The demons that possessed Mary were cast out one at a time:

"Mary had been looked upon as a great sinner, but Christ knew the circumstances that had shaped her life. . . . It was He who had lifted her from despair and ruin. *Seven times she had heard His strong cries to the Father on her behalf."* DA 568

The casting out of demons is a miracle:

" 'Master', he [John] said, 'we saw one *casting out devils in Thy name,* and he followeth not us; and we forbade him, because he followeth not us.'

"James and John had thought that in checking this man they had had in view their Lord's honor; they began to see that they were jealous of their own. They acknowledged their error, and accepted the reproof of Jesus, 'Forbid him not: for there is no man which shall *do a miracle in My name* that can lightly speak evil of Me.' " DA 437

Satan cannot force us to sin against our wills:

"While we should be keenly alive to our exposure to the assaults of unseen and invisible foes, we are to be sure that *they cannot harm us without gaining our consent*." AH 405

"No man without his own consent can be overcome by Satan. The tempter has no power to control the will or to force the soul to sin. He may distress, but he cannot contaminate. He can cause agony, but not defilement." GC 510

"I was shown that *Satan cannot control minds unless they are yielded to his control*." 1T 301

"In no case can Satan obtain dominion over the thoughts, words, and actions, unless we voluntarily open the door and invite him to enter." AH 402

We can keep Satan from gaining entrance:

"Fearful is the condition of those who resist the divine claims and yield to Satan's temptations, until God gives them up to the control of evil spirits. But *those who follow Christ are ever safe under His watchcare. Angels that excel in strength are sent from heaven to protect them. The wicked one cannot break through the guard which God has stationed about His people."* GC 517

God never ignores a cry for help:

"God does not control our minds without our consent; but every man is free to choose what power he will have to rule over him. None have fallen so low, none are so vile, but that they may find deliverance in Christ. . . . *No cry from a soul in need, though it fail of utterance in words, will be unheeded."* MH 93

"Satan and his angels are unwilling to lose their prey. They contend and battle with holy angels, and the conflict is severe. And *if those who have erred continue to plead, and in deep humility confess their wrongs, angels who excel in strength will prevail and wrench them from the power of the evil angels."* MYP 60

"Nothing is apparently more helpless, yet really more invincible, than the soul that feels its nothingness and relies wholly on the merits of the Saviour. *God would send every angel in heaven to the aid of such a one, rather than allow him to be overcome."* 7T 17

The weakest saint, with Christ, is more than a match for Satan:

"Satan is constantly at work, but few have any idea of his activity and subtlety. The people of God must be prepared to withstand the wiley foe. *It is this resistance that Satan dreads.* He knows better than we do the limit of his power and how easily he can be overcome if we resist and face him. Through divine strength *the weakest saint is more than a match for him and all his angels."* 5T 293

Satan is already a conquered foe:

"Henceforth *Christ's followers are to look upon Satan as a conquered foe. Upon the cross, Jesus was to gain the victory for them; that victory He desired them to accept as their own."* MH 94

We may have all the help that Christ had:

"The life that Christ lived in this world, men and women can live through His power and under His instruction. *In their conflict with Satan they may have all the help that He had.* They may be more than conquerors through Him who loved them and gave Himself for them." 9T 22

It is God's plan that the sick be healed and devils be cast out today:

"The church in not now the separate and peculiar people she was when the fires of persecution were kindled against her. How is the gold become dim! how is the most fine gold changed! *I saw that if the church had always retained her peculiar, holy character, the power of the Holy Spirit which was imparted to the disciples would still be with her. The sick would be healed, devils would be rebuked and cast out, and she would be mighty, and a terror to her enemies.*" EW 227

Appendix B

Some Things the Demon Said

Note: In most confrontations, we asked God to make the demons be quiet after we had learned their names and their work. However, in one encounter, when we were working with a woman other than Paula, we decided that we would not make that request, but allow the demon to talk if God permitted him to. Accordingly, we listened to him for about an hour before we decided that it would be best to ask God to keep him quiet. We came to that decision because we found ourselves increasingly tempted to seek information from him; that is, to ask questions merely out of curiosity just to see what he would say. We knew this would be wrong, and so we prayed that God would not permit him to speak further. As He always did, God answered our prayers and caused the demon to stop speaking.

We believe we have learned some things and gained some new insights since we worked with Paula. Although Jesus on at least one occasion asked the demons to identify themselves (Mark 5:9) we no longer make a practice of doing this. In more recent experiences we have asked God not to permit the demons to speak at all but to get on at once with the business of casting them out. There has been no verbal objection and much less physical action in these cases than in Paula's case. The result is that the entire experience is less exhausting physically and emotionally to everyone involved. We pray that God will give wisdom to know how to cooperate with Him in each case.

However, some of the things the demon said while he was talking were very surprising. I can account for this only by assuming that God must have caused him to make these statements, just as He caused the demon to open the door so that I could help Paula even though the demon rebuked himself later on several occasions for doing it. In the same day, the demon rebuked himself for saying some of the things he said.

Following are some of the statements made by the demon, taken from the notes I jotted down at the same time.

"I get into people when they compromise. When they don't compromise, I can't get in."

"I'm trying to destroy all the young people, all the youth. That way they can't lead any one else."

"Sometimes when she was reading the Bible, I made people call her up. They interrupted her so she could not read."

"I tried to get into your home last night. But there were too many angels around the house. I had to send for help, and even then I could not get in. You had better be careful. If I can possibly find a way, I'll get in."

"Being kind is not my nature. My nature is to kill and destroy."

"I caused the car accident you saw last night. Do you know why? So Helen could see how uncertain life is." NOTE: The previous evening there had been a bad accident not far from our home. Pastor Paddock, Helen, and I saw it a few minutes after it had happened. Helen was a girl with whom we were working.

"Why am I talking to you guys? I'm not supposed to do that. All I'm supposed to do is to destroy. Help me destroy her."

"Have you ever seen me in human form?"

"I've given you too much information. It makes me mad."

"I try to make people mad at the 'Faith for Today' program and get it off the air."

"I hate the Seventh-day Adventist Church. It has the truth."

"Jesus is coming soon."

"I've said too much today. I'm going to put a curse on all this information so that no one who heard it will believe it."

"You don't know how weak I really am."

"Noah had so much faith. He didn't even see any clouds in the sky, but he kept building the boat. I even made people laugh at him, but he just kept on building."

"Nothing is coincidental. Everything in this life is either from God or from me."

"Do you know why people lose their Christian experience? Because they don't spend enough time in prayer. They talk with me more than they do with God. That is why the Seventh-day Adventist Church is not as strong as it was. People do not pray enough."

Appendix C

Demon Possession and Its Remedy in the Bible

Mark 1:23-27: "And there was in their synagogue *a man with an unclean spirit;* and he cried out, saying, Let us alone; what have we to do with thee, thou Jesus of Nazareth? art thou come to destroy us? I know who thou art, the Holy One of God. And Jesus rebuked him, saying, Hold thy peace, and *come out of him.* And when the unclean spirit had torn him, and cried with a loud voice, he came out of him. And they were all amazed, insomuch that they questioned among themselves, saying, What is this? what new doctrine is this? for with authority commandeth he even the unclean spirits, and they do obey him." See Luke 4:33-36.

Mark 5:2-13: "And when he was come out of the ship, immediately there met him out of the tombs *a man with an unclean spirit,* who had his dwelling among the tombs; and no man could bind him, no, not with chains: because that he had been often bound with fetters and chains, and the chains had been plucked asunder by him, and the fetters broken in pieces: neither could any man tame him. And always, night and day, he was in the mountains, and in the tombs, crying and cutting himself with stones. But when he saw Jesus afar off, he ran and worshipped him, and cried with a loud voice, and said, What have I to do with thee, Jesus, thou Son of the most high God? I adjure thee by God, that thou torment me not. For he said unto him, *Come out of the man, thou unclean spirit.* And he asked him, *What is thy name? And he answered, saying, My name is Legion:* for we are many. And he besought him much that he would not send them away out of the country. Now there was nigh unto the mountains a great herd of swine feeding. And all the devils besought him, saying, Send us into the swine, that we may enter into them. And forthwith Jesus gave them leave. And the unclean spirits went out, and entered into the swine: and the herd ran violently down a steep place into the sea, (they were about two thousand;) and were choked in the sea.'' See also Luke 8:26-33.

Luke 6:17, 18: ''And he came down with them, and stood in the plain, and the company of his disciples, and a great multitude of people out of all Judaea and Jerusalem, and from the sea coast of Tyre and Sidon, which came to hear him, and to be healed of their diseases; and *they that were vexed with unclean spirits:* and they were healed.''

Luke 7:21: ''And in that same hour he cured many of their infirmities and plagues, and *of evil spirits;* and unto many that were blind he gave sight.''

Luke 8:2: ''And certain women, *which had been healed of evil spirits* and infirmities, Mary called Magdalene, out of whom went seven devils.''

Mark 7:25-30: For a certain woman, *whose young daughter had an unclean spirit,* heard of him, [Jesus] and came and fell at his feet: . . . and she besought him that he would cast forth the devil out of her daughter. . . . And he said unto her, . . . Go thy way; *the devil is gone out of thy daughter.* And when she was come to her house she found the devil gone out, and her daughter laid upon the bed.''

Matthew 12:11: "Then was brought unto him *one possessed with a devil,* blind, and dumb: and he healed him, insomuch that the blind and dumb both spake and saw."

Matthew 17:14-21: "And when they were come to the multitude, there came to him a certain man, kneeling down to him, and saying, Lord, have mercy on my son: for he is lunatick, and sore vexed: for ofttimes he falleth into the fire, and oft into the water. And I brought him to thy disciples, and they could not cure him. Then Jesus answered and said, O faithless and perverse generation, how long shall I be with you? how long shall I suffer you? Bring him hither to me. *And Jesus rebuked the devil; and he departed out of him:* and the child was cured that very hour. Then came the disciples to Jesus apart, and said, Why could we not cast him out? And Jesus said unto them, Because of your unbelief: for verily I say unto you, If ye have faith as a grain of mustard seed, ye shall say unto this mountain, Remove hence to yonder place; and it shall remove; and nothing shall be impossible unto you. However this kind goeth not out but by prayer and fasting." See Luke 9:37-42.

Note: Not only did Jesus cast out devils during His earthly ministry, but He gave power to cast out devils to the twelve disciples and to the seventy when He sent them out on their missionary tour. This power was retained by the disciples after the ascension of Christ; and Paul, after his conversion, also cast out evil spirits. See the following scriptures.

Matthew 10:1, 5-8: "And when he had called unto him his twelve disciples, *he gave them power against unclean spirits,* to cast them out, and to heal all manner of sickness and all manner of disease." "These twelve Jesus sent forth and commanded, saying, Go not into the way of the Gentiles, and into any city of the Samaritans enter ye not. But go rather to the lost sheep of the house of Israel. And as ye go, preach, saying, The kingdom of heaven is at hand. Heal the sick, cleanse the lepers, raise the dead, *cast out devils:* freely ye have received, freely give."

Luke 10:1, 17-20: "After these things the Lord appointed other seventy also, and sent them two and two before his face into every city and place, whither he himself would come." "And the seventy returned again with joy, saying, Lord, *even the devils are subject unto us through thy name.* And he said unto them, I beheld Satan as lightning fall from heaven. Behold, I give unto you power to tread on serpents and scorpions, and over all the power of the enemy: and nothing shall by any means hurt you. Notwithstanding in this *rejoice not, that the spirits are subject unto you;* but rather rejoice, because your names are written in heaven."

Mark 3:14, 15: "And he ordained twelve, that they should be with him, and that he might send them forth to preach, and to have power to heal sicknesses, and *to cast out devils."*

Mark 6:7: "And he called unto him the twelve, and began to send them forth by two and two, and *gave them power over unclean spirits . . .* "

Mark 16:17, 18: "And these signs shall follow them that believe; *In my name shall they cast out devils;* they shall speak with new tongues; they shall take up serpents; and if they drink any deadly thing, it shall not hurt them; and they shall lay hands on the sick, and they shall recover."

Acts 8:7, 8: *"For unclean spirits, crying with loud voice, came out of many that were possessed with them:* and many taken with palsies, and that were lame, were healed. And there was great joy in that city."

Acts 19:11, 12: And God wrought special miracles

by the hands of Paul: so that from his body were brought unto the sick handkerchiefs or aprons, and diseases departed from them, and *evil spirits went out of them."*

NOTE: The Scriptures depict clearly the reality and fierceness of the battle between the forces of good and evil, between Christ and His angels and Satan and his angels. But, thank God, the Scriptures also give us the assurance of victory, and they set forth the armor by whose use the victory may be gained.

1 Peter 5:8, 9: "Be sober, be vigilant; because *your adversary the devil, as a roaring lion, walketh about, seeking whom he may devour: whom resist* stedfast in the faith."

Ephesians 6:10-18: "Finally, my brethren, be strong in the Lord, and in the power of his might. *Put on the whole armour of God, that ye may be able to stand against the wiles of the devil.* For we wrestle not against flesh and blood, but against principalities, against powers, against the rulers of the darkness of this world, against spiritual wickedness in high places. *Wherefore take unto you the whole armour of God,* that ye may be able to withstand in the evil day, and having done all, to stand. Stand therefore, having your loins girt about with truth, and having on the breastplate of righteousness; and your feet shod with the preparation of the gospel of peace; above all, taking the shield of faith, wherewith ye shall be able to quench all the fiery darts of the wicked. And take the helmet of salvation, and the sword of the Spirit, which is the word of God: praying always with all prayer and supplication in the Spirit, and watching thereunto with all perseverance and supplication for all saints."

James 4:7: "*Submit* yourselves therefore to God. *Resist* the devil, and he will flee from you."

TEACH Services, Inc.
PUBLISHING

We invite you to view the complete
selection of titles we publish at:
www.TEACHServices.com

We encourage you to write us
with your thoughts about this,
or any other book we publish at:
info@TEACHServices.com

TEACH Services' titles may be purchased in
bulk quantities for educational, fund-raising,
business, or promotional use.
bulksales@TEACHServices.com

Finally, if you are interested in seeing
your own book in print, please contact us at:
publishing@TEACHServices.com
We are happy to review your manuscript at no charge.